BEGINNER'S GUIDE TO THE BIBLE'S LAST BOOK OF REVELATION AND THE SIGNIFICANCE OF THE NUMBER 7

"BLESSED IS HE THAT READETH, AND THEY THAT HEAR THE WORDS OF THIS PROPHECY, AND KEEP THOSE THINGS WHICH ARE WRITTEN THEREIN: FOR THE TIME IS AT HAND."

JOY JACOBY

WHAT I AM GRATEFUL FOR

> *Blessed is he that readeth, and they that hear the words of this prophecy, and keep those things which are written therein: for the time is at hand.*
>
> — *KING JAMES BIBLE*, 2017/1611, REVELATION 1:3

When I look at how far God has taken me and where He has brought me from, I have to dedicate this book to God for being a faithful father to me. We often don't recognize how much we need a father to guide us through life until we come to realize how lost we truly are. For those of us who were fortunate enough to grow up with their biological father, you can understand what it's like to have someone be your eyes and ears in a world filled with so much darkness. And that's also the reason why I'm thankful to God for sending His son Jesus Christ who is the light in the darkness and has washed away our sins. I may never fully understand His importance in my life, but I can be certain in saying that without Him, my life would be void.

Aside from God and Jesus Christ as the source of all things good in my life, I also want to acknowledge the few people who have helped me in my journey to draw closer to the Savior. Heading the list is Father Terry Keenan who, despite knowing of my divorce, still invited me to his parish at Holy Family Church in Inverness, Illinois. According to the Catholic faith, being divorced prohibits a person from receiving holy communion. But Father Keenan responded in a very compassionate way, ensuring me that *all* are welcome at the Lord's table, which is an excellent example of God's heart toward us.

This is precisely the reason why Jesus gave Himself on the cross: to save the sinners and those in need of deliverance. With such a beautiful reminder, I've felt welcome to partake in communion with the Lord Jesus Christ without the fear of rejection. While there are standards to living the life of a believer in Christ, it doesn't help to constantly highlight the sins or shortcomings of others. That's not the message of Christ, and it's definitely not how He drew followers to Himself.

I'm also grateful for the counsel of Pastor Jack Hibbs who is a pastor at Calvary Chapel in Chino Hills, California. I'm a follower of his on YouTube and have been closely listening to him for many years now—to be honest, for several times each week, which mainly consists of his Wednesday Bible study service and his many services on Sundays. I especially like the fact that he keeps things interesting by allowing different speakers to take the stage. It does a great job of providing unique perspectives and broadening the understanding of the viewers, myself included!

Through watching Pastor Jack Hibbs, I have been exposed to Amir Tsarfati, who is a Jewish author, Israeli public figure, and Middle East news commentator. Although he is a Jew, he has accepted Jesus Christ as his Lord and Savior and currently lives in Jerusalem where he diligently keeps the world posted on what's happening in the country, especially as we know its significance in Bible prophecy. We should all be continuing to pray for Jerusalem as we head into greater manifestations of the Book of Revelation.

Finally, this book is dedicated to America! The country that I love and cherish for the fact that it was founded on God and liberty, the two things that seem to be under attack in America and the entire world. All who look upon America can agree that it is floundering into a cesspool of debauchery and untamed sin. Schools have fought to remove God and prayer in schools, people's liberties to preach the gospel are being withstood, and there is even corruption in the churches themselves. It's become obvious that we need God to restore His blessings upon us. But there is a stipulation, and I believe it includes repenting and returning to the Lord.

The lyrics of the song "America the Beautiful" share how blessed we have been as a nation. And despite the chastisement, we're still being blessed! So please, pray that God once again has mercy and sheds "His grace on thee and crown thy good with brotherhood from sea to shining sea."

CONTENTS

INTRODUCTION TO GOD'S REVELATION

> *He will wipe every tear from their eyes. There will be no more death or mourning or crying or pain, for the old order of things has passed away.*
>
> — *NEW INTERNATIONAL VERSION*, 2011, REVELATION 21:4

Have you ever been kept up at night rattling your brain and exercising every ounce of discernment you have trying to decipher the Book of Revelation? Has it ever occurred to you why this book is the most intriguing book of the Bible to most believers, and yet so few take the time to study it in depth because of how confusing its contents seem to be? While you may be met with far more questions than answers upon the call to go into depth with the study of this magnificent portion of the Scripture, it's a step in the right direction if you hope to become a seasoned Christian.

Even more importantly, with all the uncertainty going on in the world now more than ever, people are anxious, curious, fearful, and in need of direction. And with so many questionable church doctrines floating around today, believers in Christ are all the more interested in reading and applying the Word of God to their lives on a more personal level. Did you know that the title of the book, Revelation, is derived from the Greek word for apocalypse, which is *apokálypsis*, and refers to an "uncovering" or an unveiling of something that is unknown?

And so this "revealing" or "disclosure" of things not yet known is what makes the title of the Book of Revelation so fitting as its writing is highly prophetic and focuses on things that are to come in the future. Rife with scriptures of otherworldly imagery and vivid depictions of the rise and fall of an Antichrist system, it's not all doom and gloom with the last book of the Bible. Though many of the prophecies concern war, famine, and a time of tribulation unlike any other time in history, there are also promises of a new heaven and a new earth where the righteous kingdom of God reigns with Jesus Christ as the governing authority over all.

Further historic facts surrounding the Book of Revelation reveal that it was written by the Apostle John in the year 95 while he was exiled on the Greek island of Patmos, located off the coast of Asia Minor, which is modern-day Turkey. Experts reveal that John was sent there as a form of punishment after the ruling Roman emperor ordered him to be burned alive in hot oil as a means of torture and death, but his life was preserved by God miraculously.

It was during his exile in solitude on the island of Patmos that the entire Book of Revelation came to John during a vision, which is possibly the reason why the literature was filled with such dramatic imagery, making it seem difficult for the readers to understand.

Knowing that you are living in the last days is already a tough pill to swallow, but accepting the reality that there are still incredibly tumultuous times ahead can be a truth that many openly resist. It seems like things can't possibly get worse than they already are—rising gas prices, inflation, globally impacting pestilences and diseases, the love of mankind growing cold, and a lack of trust in political and religious powers—the list is seemingly endless.

But there is a saying that it's always darkest before dawn. So despite the hopelessness the world is facing, the Book of Revelation is actually a story about God's blueprint for the Second Coming of Christ and the final punishment of Satan and his cohorts in the lake of fire. There are promises of protection and provision; an end to distress, pain, sorrow, death, and darkness; as well as everlasting life in eternal glory for overcoming the mark of the beast and the worship of the Antichrist.

Suffice it to say that even as believers will be going through intense tribulation on earth during this time, they won't have to wait to be martyred or wisped off to heaven in some other way to experience the manifest promises of God. If you're on the winning team of Jesus, there will be many victories to be experienced during such an exciting period in biblical history!

But this is precisely the reason why the *Beginner's Guide to the Bible's Last Book of Revelation* is so necessary for the believer living in the last days before Christ's prophesied return. Surely, you are aware that you will be protected as the Messiah has promised to do so even until the end of the age, but having greater clarity on the sequence of events that have taken and will take place will put you in a position of readiness.

The Bible says in the Book of Matthew 24:42 that we should, "Therefore keep watch, because you do not know on what day your Lord will come." While it is true that we will not know the exact day, there will be signs that point to the season we are in so that the day of His coming will not come upon us like a thief in the night.

The purpose of this book is to take you step by step through the Book of Revelation as it highlights many of the signs that you should be looking for. You will be given access to a thorough breakdown of each chapter as it progresses to the glorious victory that you as a believer are inherited to receive. Due to the fact that the entire Book of Revelation is basically the interpretations of a series of profound visions communicated to a man thousands of years ago, some of the wording may be difficult to deduce.

That's why this book will make it easily digestible, especially for believers mustering the courage to delve into such an intimidating book of the Bible. And it's equally useful in bringing an unbeliever into the fold of Christ. The reality of such historic events happening in our time is enough to make you want to get on the winning team with Jesus and partake in the priceless gift of eternal life.

Blessed with a rich background in the Methodist, Lutheran, and Catholic denominations, Joy has garnered decades of wisdom from different perspectives and doctrines, which has given her a truly unique perspective on the Book of Revelation. Learning the things of God through the trials of life is never easy, but it is completely necessary if you plan on using the wisdom learned on that journey to inspire others.

Get excited! Because if you're a lover of knowledge and unfiltered truth, then the contents of this book are exactly what you've been looking for. As we all ride these turbulent waves of life into the great and perfect day of Christ's return, rest assured that you will be guided correctly all the way into those pearly white gates of heaven. There are mysteries in the Book of Revelation that you won't believe existed, but you'll have to continue reading to find out for yourself!

1

REVELATION 1—THE KINGDOM OF GOD IS NEAR

REVELATION 1:1–20

Prologue

The revelation from Jesus Christ, which God gave him to show his servants what must soon take place. He made it known by sending his angel to his servant John, who testifies to everything he saw—that is, the word of God and the testimony of Jesus Christ. Blessed is the one who reads aloud the words of this prophecy, and blessed are those who hear it and take to heart what is written in it, because the time is near.

Greetings and Doxology

John, To the seven churches in the province of Asia: Grace and peace to you from him who is, and who was, and who is to come, and from the seven spirits before his throne, and from Jesus Christ, who is the faithful witness, the firstborn from the dead, and the ruler of the kings of the earth. To him who loves us and has freed us from our sins by his blood, and has made us to be a kingdom and priests to serve his God and Father—to him be glory and power for ever and ever! Amen. "Look, he is coming with the clouds," and "every eye will see him, even those who pierced him"; and all peoples on earth "will mourn because of him." So shall it be! Amen. "I am the Alpha and the Omega," says the Lord God, "who is, and who was, and who is to come, the Almighty."

John's Vision of Christ

I, John, your brother and companion in the suffering and kingdom and patient endurance that are ours in Jesus, was on the island of Patmos because of the word of God and the testimony of Jesus. On the Lord's Day I was in the Spirit, and I heard behind me a loud voice like a trumpet, which said: "Write on a scroll what you see and send it to the seven churches: to Ephesus, Smyrna, Pergamum, Thyatira, Sardis, Philadelphia and Laodicea." I turned around to see the voice that was speaking to me. And when I turned I saw seven golden lampstands, and among the lampstands was someone like a son of man, dressed in a robe reaching down to his feet and with a golden sash around his chest. The hair on his head was white like wool, as white as snow, and his eyes were like blazing fire. His feet were like bronze glowing in a furnace, and his voice was like the sound of rushing waters. In his right hand he held seven stars, and coming out of his mouth was a sharp, double-edged sword. His face was

> like the sun shining in all its brilliance. When I saw him, I fell at his feet as though dead. Then he placed his right hand on me and said: "Do not be afraid. I am the First and the Last. I am the Living One; I was dead, and now look, I am alive for ever and ever! And I hold the keys of death and Hades. "Write, therefore, what you have seen, what is now and what will take place later. The mystery of the seven stars that you saw in my right hand and of the seven golden lampstands is this: The seven stars are the angels of the seven churches, and the seven lampstands are the seven churches.

Revelation 1:1–3 Revealed

Firstly, to properly understand the Book of Revelation, one would need to consider how the first book of the Bible, Genesis, explains creation and the fall of man, followed by the other 65 books that explain the redemption of man through the stories of the patriarchs and promise of Christ's coming. Finally, the 66th book of the Bible, the Book of Revelation, delivers the climactic conclusion of Christ coming back as the lion of the tribe of Judah to make an end of the Antichrist and his kingdom and establish His own kingdom on a new earth.

One of the biggest controversies about the Bible is the fact that people tend to have their own methods of interpretation. The influence of a person's denomination or personal biases may play a major part in the way they perceive each verse. Because of this reality, there are certain ways of thinking that should be avoided when studying or interpreting the deeper mysteries of the Book of Revelation. These include the following:

- isolating the scriptures in the Book of Revelation from other books in the Bible
- assuming or guessing the interpretation of more ambiguous texts
- pretending to know or understand the meaning of a scripture instead of admitting ignorance
- rejecting new information because it sounds foreign or doesn't line up with traditional ways of thinking

On the contrary, as we begin to dive into the Scripture, the golden rule of sorts for interpreting scriptures is to accept when a text makes common sense instead of intentionally mystifying an otherwise plain, forthright meaning. Scriptures often tend to become totally misconstrued because of this, leading to more confusion. And we know that God is not the author of confusion. Let's cover a few other rules you can apply when studying the Scripture:

- Take the text at its simplest form until it is proven otherwise.
- Seek to understand the text in the way the author intended it.
- Don't dismiss the real meaning of a text because it may seem far-fetched or extraordinary.
- Resist the urge to over-spiritualize a straightforward text of a scripture, which can result in the wrong interpretation.

As we begin to uncover the truth even from the first chapter of Revelation, you'll notice the use of a great deal of symbolism, as they are also present in other areas of the Bible as well. Deciphering the meaning of symbolism may seem like a daunting task especially for passages that are over 2,000 years old. According to Verse by Verse Ministry International (2019a), the meaning of the symbol is usually found in the immediate text. On occasions where the immediate text doesn't provide answers, go backward in the book to find the answer.

If the interpretation cannot be found in the same book, perhaps scanning through the previous books of the Scripture will prove to be successful.

With that being said, we'll apply this blueprint to the first three verses of the first chapter, namely, Revelation 1:1–3:

> The revelation from Jesus Christ, which God gave him to show his servants what must soon take place. He made it known by sending his angel to his servant John, who testifies to everything he saw—that is, the word of God and the testimony of Jesus Christ. Blessed is the one who reads aloud the words of this prophecy, and blessed are those who hear it and take to heart what is written in it, because the time is near.

The Letter, the Author, and the Audience

Like other books in the Bible, the Book of Revelation is described as a letter which is being communicated to John by an angel, or a messenger, and then to be delivered to a wider audience.

The first verse of Chapter 1 gives the reader a few important clues about who is delivering the message. The very first words of the verse include the words "Revelation of Jesus Christ." The word revelation in Greek means "apocalypse." So we can suggest that the "Revelation of Jesus Christ" is truly apocalyptic in nature.

Telling from the heavy use of symbolism and John's desperate attempt to relay the troubling visions he was receiving, you can clearly see that he was trying to describe the events from visions that revealed a time far beyond his present era.

Also, bear in mind that there is no other letter in the New Testament that is regarded as being the true revelation of Jesus Christ. Earlier books of the New Testament, such as Matthew, Luke, Mark, and John, all highlighted the birth of Christ, His early life and earthly ministry, and all the way to His ultimate betrayal on the cross of Calvary where He became the ultimate lamb sacrifice whose blood had to be shed for the remission of our sins.

So the Book of Revelation is truly unique in that it is describing the revelation of Jesus Christ who is now reigning as the King of kings on heaven's throne beside His Father and will be coming back as the lion of the tribe of Judah to make a complete end of Satan and the kingdoms of men that are currently governing this world system. What an exciting time to be alive!

After declaring this to be the revelation of Jesus Christ, verse 1 goes on to confirm who the revelation came from, implying that "God" (meaning the Father of Christ) gave Him. Herein we see the chain of command from the Father to the Son, meaning that this book was given to Christ by His heavenly Father. But it doesn't stop there.

This book, like every teaching that Christ delivered, was meant to be given to His bond servants. Who are the bond servants of Christ, you ask? A bond servant, in its literal meaning, is a slave. However, in the New Testament, it's a term that is used to represent the followers of Jesus Christ.

Revelation 1:1 further makes it clear that the letter being given to the servants is to inform them of things that must shortly take place. And while this book was written by John in 96, the word "shortly" seems questionable. But there is no denying the fact that we're seeing a massive increase in the fulfillment of the prophecies from the Book of Revelation in modern times.

You would think that the chain of custody from the Father, to the Son, and to the followers of Jesus Christ is all there was to it. But there is still a missing link that we can't ignore—the angels.

The Angel Delivers the Message

The angel prepares to communicate the details of the letter to John, who we can assume is John the apostle whom Christ loved, since the Scripture does not suggest otherwise. However, even with the trusted character of Apostle John, the chain of custody was extremely important since there were many false teachings regarding the return of Jesus, as there are today. So in order for the validity of the testimony to be accepted by the church, it had to come from Jesus' angel, who received it from Jesus Himself, who got it from the source—His Father.

John "Saw" the Revelation of Jesus Christ

Verse 2 states, "who testifies to everything he saw—that is, the word of God and the testimony of Jesus Christ."

This clearly signifies that what was described by words were actually the details of events John saw. The truth of this is confirmed in verse

1 where it is understood that Jesus "shows" the revelations to his bond servants. This also helps to put into perspective the confusion that many believers report when reading the Book of Revelation, since they are reading the attempted written narrative of what John saw.

Undoubtedly, John didn't know some of the things he was shown, and so his descriptions may seem incomprehensible. But this is where the Holy Spirit comes into play, as He would help to interpret the verses for the believer, while remaining obscure to the unbeliever.

Incentive for the Believer

For the believers who are hesitant to read and/or study the Book of Revelation, verse 3 gives you an incentive by ensuring a blessing to whoever reads, hears, and heeds the prophecy communicated in the book. To take "heed" means to give great consideration by believing what the book is revealing as true.

Understanding the importance of this book for the last days, Christ must've thought to give believers a blessing to encourage them to read and study for themselves despite the intimidating nature of the book. But now that we've covered the first three verses of Chapter 1, let's continue to verse 4.

Revelation 1:4–8 Revealed

As we've established, Apostle John is the author of the letter. He is basically the writing vessel through whom Jesus writes down every word verbatim to be sent to the seven churches in Asia. Here is the first place in the Book of Revelation where you may begin to frequently use the number "seven," and the coming chapters will quickly confirm this.

Certain numbers are used repeatedly throughout the Bible, which means they have some level of significance. Here are a few places in the Bible where number seven is used:

- the completion of God's creation on the seventh day, in which He rested, leading to the Sabbath (Genesis 2:2)
- sevenfold vengeance from God upon Cain for killing Abel (Genesis 4:15)
- seven pairs of every clean animal packed into the ark of Noah (Genesis 7:2)
- seven years of plenty and seven years of famine for Egypt in Pharaoh's dream (Genesis 41)
- seven days of the Passover feast (Exodus 13:3–10)

Using these examples, we see that God has ascribed a certain meaning to the number seven, which is completion. The number seven is the Bible's way of saying that something is complete, whole, or perfect. Therefore, the use of the number seven when speaking of the churches which are in Asia means that Christ was referring to the entire church throughout history. Surely, there were way more than seven churches in Asia at the time.

You will find the use of the number seven again later in the same verse when it mentions the seven spirits before the throne, which are the seven spirits of God. According to Riggleman (2022), the following are the seven spirits of God:

1. the Spirit of wisdom
2. the Spirit of the Lord
3. the Spirit of understanding
4. the Spirit of counsel
5. the Spirit of power
6. the Spirit of knowledge
7. the Spirit of the fear of the Lord

Verse 5 then addresses Jesus as the faithful witness, the firstborn from the dead, and the ruler of the kings of the earth. These names are assigned to Christ to signify the three periods of Jesus' ministry throughout biblical history as the second person of the Godhead.

- In Colossians 1:16, Paul describes how Christ is the one true witness who beheld the existence of God through the creation before He manifested in the flesh, stating that "all things have been created through him and for him."
- Paul also goes on to explain how He is the firstborn from the dead in Colossians 1:18.
- Since Jesus is known as the one who was, is, and is to come, His Second Coming to earth will mark the third period of His ministry where He will rule as the King of kings. 1 Peter 2:9 calls the believers "a chosen people, a royal priesthood," which means that we are the kings and priests who will be reigning under Christ in the kingdom to come. Although right now, we serve as priests (or intercessors) who have been freed from sin by the blood of Jesus and stand in the gap for the lost in hopes that they will come to Him.

Paul also goes on to explain how He is the firstborn from the dead in Colossians 1:18. Since Jesus is known as the one who was, is, and is to come, His Second Coming to earth will mark the third period of His ministry where He will rule as the King of kings.

Revelation 1:9–16 Revealed

The author of the passage clears up any lingering suspicion of his true identity as the Apostle Paul by calling himself "your brother" and fellow partaker in the persecutions and tribulations of the early church. Further evidence proving that Apostle John is the author is his mention in verse 9 of being isolated in the island of Patmos because of his faith in Jesus.

There are historic records detailing the exile of John to the island by the Romans after failing to kill him by plunging him into boiling oil. Records also have it that John ministered in Ephesus, which isn't far from Patmos. You will also see that Ephesus is among one of the seven churches John mentions.

It is said that John was in his early 80s when he wrote the Book of Revelation. Early church fathers also believe that after the death of Emperor Domitian, John was freed from Patmos and returned to Ephesus where he delivered his letter to the church, making it available to us even today.

In verse 10, John says, "I was in the Spirit" on the "Lord's day," signifying the depth of prayer he was engaged in. He then heard a loud voice like that of a trumpet, which later became more intelligible speech. The loud voice then gives him a set of directives to follow:

- John is told to write a book of what he "sees" and send it to the seven churches, which are Ephesus, Smyrna, Pergamum, Thyatira, Sardis, Philadelphia, and Laodicea.
- Again, we see that John is to write what he sees, not what he hears.

John's Vision of the Seven Golden Lampstands

After being completely dumbfounded by the blast of the trumpet, John turns to behold Christ speaking to him in the form of a golden lampstand with seven branches. The type of lampstand he saw was akin to the seven-branched lampstand God commanded Israel to construct for the tabernacle.

Notice again the use of the number seven reminding us of the completion that's taking place in the Book of Revelation.

Upon closer inspection, John sees standing in the middle of the lampstand "one like a son of man" which is a phrase used to represent Christ, although it isn't made clear that it is Jesus. John gives further detail about the manly figure, highlighting that he saw him "dressed in a robe reaching down to his feet and with a golden sash around his chest" (verse 13). Features such as these describe someone who has authority like a priest or king. These are features attributed to Christ, but again, that isn't confirmed.

More Details About Appearance

Revelation 1:14 goes into more detail about the appearance of the manly figure in the middle of the golden lampstand:

- Further description says that His head and hair were white like wool or snow, with eyes like a flame of fire.
- His feet were described as appearing like burnished bronze, red and glowing.
- His voice is described as having the sound of many waters, like a raging waterfall.
- John reports the figure holding seven stars in one hand with a two-edged sword protruding out of His mouth.
- His face is shining brightly like the sun.

You should've noticed a similarity in the number of stars being seven, denoting the number of perfection and completion. The following verse explains the symbolism.

Revelation 1:17–20 Revealed

The last three verses continue with Revelation 1:17 in which John describes falling at the feet of Jesus as a dead man after what he witnessed. By saying, "I fell at his feet as though dead," implies the sheer dread and terror that John felt, enough to immobilize him. The presence and power of God tends to have this effect on mankind, as we can see in Joshua 5:13–14 and Daniel 8:17. One would think that John, who was Jesus' closest disciple, would be ecstatic to see his Savior. But clearly, Jesus' appearance was different from what John was used to, hence the similarity in his response to Joshua, Daniel, and other prophets who saw Christ in His glory.

Recognizing John's fear, Jesus seeks to comfort him by telling him not to be afraid and describes Himself as being the first, the last, the living one, and the one who was dead and is alive forevermore.

With that, Jesus (*Yeshua*) then charges John in Revelation 1:19 to "write, therefore, what you have seen, what is now and what will take place later." Since Christ is omniscient and omnipresent, He switches from present tense, to past tense, and to future tense all in the same sentence.

The final verse in the first chapter, Revelation 1:20, is where Jesus reveals to John "the mystery of the seven stars that you saw in my right hand and of the seven golden lampstands." He goes on to explain that "the seven stars are the angels of the seven churches, and the seven lampstands are the seven churches." So here, you can clearly see how symbols are used to represent other things entirely.

Notice the use of the number seven yet again. Jesus is driving home the idea that He is planning to wrap things up with the constant use of number seven.

The Book of Hebrews 1:14 says, "Are not all angels ministering spirits sent to serve those who will inherit salvation?"

The angels appear to be serving in the churches under Jesus' control as some sort of surveillance, giving Christ access to see what the state of each church is. We can say that He walks through the churches using the angels and is able to oversee, minister, and rule it from His throne in heaven.

Congrats! You've covered Chapter 1 of the Book of Revelation! The next chapter will be going more into detail about the seven churches.

End-of-Chapter Quiz

1. On which Greek island did John write the Book of Revelation?
2. Why was John sent to be exiled on the island to begin with?
3. How was the Book of Revelation communicated to John?
4. How many times is the number seven used in the first chapter of Revelation?
5. Who is the Book of Revelation being written for?

Answers

1. Revelation 1:9 tells us that John was on the Greek island of Patmos.
2. Revelation 1:9 also reveals that John was exiled on Patmos as punishment for the Word of God and the testimony of Jesus Christ.
3. An angel was sent to communicate the letters to John in the form of a vision.
4. The number seven was referenced three times in Revelation Chapter 1.
5. According to Revelation 1:1, the book was being written by John to show the servants of Christ a series of prophetic events.

2

REVELATION 2—THE SEVEN CHURCHES

REVELATION 2:1–29

To the Church in Ephesus

To the angel of the church in Ephesus write: These are the words of him who holds the seven stars in his right hand and walks among the seven golden lampstands. I know your deeds, your hard work and your perseverance. I know that you cannot tolerate wicked people, that you have tested those who claim to be apostles but are not, and have found them false. You have persevered and have endured hardships for my name, and have not grown weary. Yet I hold this against you: You have forsaken the love you had at first. Consider how far you have fallen! Repent and do the things you did at first. If you do not repent, I will come to you and remove your lampstand from its place. But you have this in your favor: You hate the practices of the Nicolaitans, which I also hate. Whoever has ears, let them hear what the Spirit says to the churches. To the one who is victorious, I will give the right to eat from the tree of life, which is in the paradise of God.

To the Church in Smyrna

To the angel of the church in Smyrna write: These are the words of him who is the First and the Last, who died and came to life again. I know your afflictions and your poverty —yet you are rich! I know about the slander of those who say they are Jews and are not, but are a synagogue of Satan. Do not be afraid of what you are about to suffer. I tell you, the devil will put some of you in prison to test you, and you will suffer persecution for ten days. Be faithful, even to the point of death, and I will give you life as your victor's crown. Whoever has ears, let them hear what the Spirit says to the churches. The one who is victorious will not be hurt at all by the second death.

To the Church in Pergamum

To the angel of the church in Pergamum write: These are the words of him who has the sharp, double-edged sword. I know where you live—where Satan has his throne. Yet you remain true to my name. You did not renounce your faith in me, not even in the days of Antipas, my faithful witness, who was put to death in your city—where Satan lives. Nevertheless, I have a few things against you: There are some among you who hold to the teaching of Balaam, who taught Balak to entice the Israelites to sin so that they ate food sacrificed to idols and committed sexual immorality.

Likewise, you also have those who hold to the teaching of the Nicolaitans. Repent therefore! Otherwise, I will soon come to you and will fight against them with the sword of my mouth. Whoever has ears, let them hear what the Spirit says to the churches. To the one who is victorious, I will give some of the hidden manna. I will also give that person a white stone with a new name written on it, known only to the one who receives it.

To the Church in Thyatira

To the angel of the church in Thyatira write: These are the words of the Son of God, whose eyes are like blazing fire and whose feet are like burnished bronze. I know your deeds, your love and faith, your service and perseverance, and that you are now doing more than you did at first. Nevertheless, I have this against you: You tolerate that woman Jezebel, who calls herself a prophet. By her teaching she misleads my servants into sexual immorality and the eating of food sacrificed to idols. I have given her time to repent of her immorality, but she is unwilling. So I will cast her on a bed of suffering, and I will make those who commit adultery with her suffer intensely, unless they repent of her ways. I will strike her children dead. Then all the churches will know that I am he who searches hearts and minds, and I will repay each of you according to your deeds. Now I say to the rest of you in Thyatira, to you who do not hold to her teaching and have not learned Satan's so-called deep secrets, 'I will not impose any other burden on you, except to hold on to what you have until I come.' To the one who is victorious and does my will to the end, I will give authority over the nations

> —that one 'will rule them with an iron scepter and will dash them to pieces like pottery'—just as I have received authority from my Father. I will also give that one the morning star. Whoever has ears, let them hear what the Spirit says to the churches.

Revelation 2:1–7 Revealed

As we stated previously, there are a total of seven churches each bearing the name of a city. For each city mentioned, Jesus greets them with a salutation before serving them either an acclamation, a condemnation, an exhortation, a promise, or a warning. As each church is being covered, it will be made clear that they are not only being discussed from a literal and historical perspective but a prophetic and eschatological perspective as well.

The Church of Ephesus

First on the list of churches is Ephesus. Geographically, Ephesus was a port city located on the Mediterranean Sea and was a very wealthy city due to the flow of goods through the seaport connecting the eastern and western end of the Roman Empire. The church at Ephesus was regarded as one of the largest and most influential churches of the first century, with some of the champions of the faith like Paul, John, and Timothy presiding as leaders over that city for years.

Despite the gospel of Christ being preached, the city was still inundated with vices like prostitution and goddess worship, being that its largest temple was set up for the praise of Artemis and Diana.

Jesus continues the verse by addressing Himself as the one with the seven stars in His hand, walking among the seven golden lampstands, as described in the previous chapter.

- The reason behind why He used the stars and the golden lampstand as symbols is because, as we learned, the stars in Revelation represent the angels sent by Christ to minister to the saints.
- He used the lampstand to symbolize the church's role as the light in the midst of a dark world through preaching the truth of Jesus Christ. The imagery of Him standing or "walking" in the midst of the seven lampstands implies His authority over the church—a gentle reminder of who's still in charge.

Moving onto Revelation 2:2–3, Jesus congratulates this church body on their good deeds, hard work, perseverance, and intolerance for false apostles and evil men. The apostles of Christ, such as John and the other 11 disciples, were handpicked by Jesus and given special powers. But many men began to falsely claim to be apostles in their lust for positions of power, and the church of Ephesus was sure to screen them. When these men couldn't perform the miraculous signs and power that true apostles exhibit, they were cast out of the church.

He continues to commend the church for their perseverance in the faith and for not growing weary despite the many oppositions they have to face. These verses can be applied in the lives of believers today because there are still many false brethren, pastors, deacons, bishops, and teachers who have crept their way into positions of power in churches either for financial increase or simply to introduce doctrines of devils. Believers are to test the spirit of even their church leaders before blindly submitting.

Leaving Their First Love

In Revelation 2:4–5, after stating the deeds that He is pleased with, Jesus gives the church of Ephesus an admonition for having left their first love, who is Christ Himself. While such a claim seems counterintuitive for a church that was so discerning and unwavering in their faith and good deeds, Christ nevertheless pointed out the flaw.

Based on the contents of the letter, we see that Christ has to remind them that He has the authority to remove their lampstand from its place if they do not repent for where they have fallen short. It then becomes clear that while the church of Ephesus was resistant to the false apostles, they also became resistant to the rulership of Christ over His church.

They became so consumed with performing good deeds that they lost sight of their Savior, and their actions were no longer motivated by their love for Christ. They may have come to depend on their good deeds as a measure for their righteousness, which then takes the focus off of Christ.

This behavior can also be seen in the modern church, where Christians become self-satisfied with keeping up the routine of going to church on Sundays, reciting the same prayers, singing the same hymns, and listening to a stale sermon from their preacher. They have made this a part of their life's schedule while neglecting to make Christ the Lord of their lives. Over time, such a mundane form of discipleship is bound to douse the flame of love that you once had for Jesus. Soon enough, you probably won't be led by the spirit of God anymore which will cause your Christian walk to seem boring and uneventful.

Christ didn't want that for His church nor does He want it for believers today. That's the reason He gave such a stern warning to repent, lest He remove their lampstand and they cease to be a church any longer. However, the one thing that Jesus says He favors about them is their hatred for the Nicolaitans, which He also shares, as stated in verse 6.

But who were the Nicolaitans? According to Verse by Verse Ministry International (2019b), the name means "victorious over the people," alluding to a movement to conquer the church congregation. Many scholars believe that the Nicolaitans were a ruling class in the church responsible for introducing heresy. Others believe that the sect that was formed after Nicolah, after whom the group is named, was one of the early church deacons in the Book of Acts that later became an apostate, teaching a perverted doctrine of grace and indulgence.

In Revelation 2:7, Christ gives a promise for those who have ears to "hear what the Spirit says to the churches" that they will eat of the tree of life. These are words of encouragement that Christ gives to the believers at the end of every letter. You will realize the same pattern of encouragement at the end of all the letters.

Revelation 2:8–29 Revealed

Although the letters were written over 2,000 years ago and refer to the surrounding churches at that time, they are very much prophetic and are meant to be decoded by the believers who would be alive at the end of the church age. Every detail in the Book of Revelation, no matter how catastrophic, is a part of God's plan. And this is where the faith and perseverance of the saints will be tested.

Now, we're going to decipher the letter to the church at Smyrna. Let's start decoding!

The Church of Smyrna

The second Roman city is called Smyrna and is the transliteration from the Greek word *smurna*, meaning the fragrant ointment called myrrh. Myrrh was one of the main embalming spices used to prepare dead bodies, which associates it with death and burial. Although it is still a thriving city today in Turkey called Izmir, it was full of pagan temples from Jesus' time and was known as the heart of emperor worship. Roman law enforced emperor worship, and Smyrna soon became the capital for such practices in Asia Minor, which in turn led to the persecution of Christians.

Jesus begins verse 8 by describing Himself as "the First and the Last, who died and came to life again." This verse sets the pace for what Christ says next that He knows the works, tribulation, and poverty of the church of Smyrna. This lets you know that the church seems to be in poverty and tribulation because they are being persecuted, and some will be destined for death.

This was, of course, connected to their faith in Christ, since both the Jews and the Romans opposed Christianity. The Romans controlled the trade unions and worshiped pagan gods that required ritual sacrifice, so Christians who did not serve their gods were automatically unable to work.

Following that, He condemns the blasphemy of those who call themselves Jews but are truly the synagogue of Satan. This would be accurate if they are working together with the Romans to persecute the believers in Christ. Although Jesus Himself is of Jewish descent, He has made a clear distinction regarding those who are Jews only by name but reject Him as the promised Messiah.

- This is similar to what He said in John 8:44 when addressing the Jews, "You belong to your father, the devil, and you want to carry out your father's desires. He was a murderer from the beginning, not holding to the truth, for there is no truth in him."
- A similar reference is also made in 1 John 2:22 which says, "Who is the liar? It is whoever denies that Jesus is the Christ. Such a person is the antichrist—denying the Father and the Son."

Despite their outward poverty, Christ assures them that they are indeed rich but in eternal blessings. As Christ said, it is better to store up your treasures in heaven where no rust will form nor can it be stolen, because heavenly rewards far outweigh any earthly benefits.

In Revelation 2:10, the church is reminded not to fear the things they are suffering and will suffer, such as imprisonment and even death. Since Christians were considered criminals because of their faith, they would be punished either by imprisonment, scourging, or death depending on the severity of the crime. The Romans would not profit from housing prisoners for long periods since they would be giving free food and clothing to so-called criminals. Therefore, 10 days would be the time limit to house a prisoner until a final verdict was made.

The death penalty for "more serious" crimes done by believers meant they would be fed to the lions in the Roman amphitheater, which even Apostle Paul experienced, as he reported in 2 Timothy 4:17. Jesus comforts the persecuted church by assuring them a crown of life if they are faithful unto death.

A crown in the New Testament is indicative of a reward for good performance or good deeds in serving Christ. This is not to be mistaken with salvation, which is a free gift of God that cannot be earned by earthly efforts. Instead, the crown of life spoken of in verse 10 is reserved for those who faithfully endure persecution, even to the point of death.

That being said, we conclude the second letter which is characterized by a period of persecution. Let's begin the third letter.

Church of Pergamum

To better understand why Christ admonishes the church of Pergamum in Revelation 2:12, you'll need to understand the definition of the city named Pergamum. The name comes from the two Greek words *pergos*, which means a "tower," and *gamos* which means "matrimony" (Verse by Verse Ministry International, 2019c). Together, Pergamum means "married to a powerful institution," and it lived up to its name as one of the most powerful cities in the Roman province.

Christ even says in Revelation 2:13, "I know thy works, and where thou dwellest, even where Satan's seat is." He made such a bold statement because the city was a Hellenistic cesspool littered with pagan temples and cults dedicated to other gods such as Zeus and Dionysus. Keep in mind that Christ is speaking to a church of believers who live among such bold evil practices. He goes on to say that despite their surroundings, the church has still called on His name and kept the faith in the face of persecution.

Jesus then likens their faith to a faithful believer named Antipas who lived in Pergamum and is assumed to have been martyred for his faith in Christ and opposition of pagan practices.

After listing their commendable qualities, the Messiah begins to proclaim their shortcomings in Revelation 2:14. He admonishes some in the church for following the teachings of Balaam, who by the way, was an Old Testament character who traded his office as a prophet to God to satisfy his greed. Christ simply used him to describe the state of the believers in Pergamum, who also traded their faithfulness to God for money and worldly possessions.

Balaam's greed led to corruption and accepted a bribe that would cause the children of Israel to commit sexual immorality and sacrifice to idols, the latter being a form of spiritual prostitution. There were some teachers in the church of Pergamos who were exhibiting those same behaviors, and there are many doing the same today.

In verse 15, we see the Nicolaitans mentioned again when Christ says that in addition to the doctrine of Balaam, there are believers who also hold to the doctrine of the Nicolaitans, which He hates. He abhors the false teachings of Balaam and the Nicolaitans so much because they pervert the pure doctrine of Christ and encourage believers to live for their flesh instead of living in the Spirit.

The false teachings of Balaam and the Nicolaitans were designed to manipulate Christians into a life of fleshly living. Being the good shepherd He is, Jesus must correct this heresy before all His sheep are led astray. As a result, He gives a command and a warning in Revelation 2:16 that those who teach and follow such false teachings must repent. Refusal to repent will cause Him to fight against them with the sword of His mouth, which is the Word of God. It's only right that Jesus, who is the manifest Word of God, uses the true doctrine of God's Word to correct all false teachings.

Church of Thyatira

The description Christ gives of Himself in Revelation 2:18 is quite intense, showing Himself as "the Son of God, whose eyes are like blazing fire and whose feet are like burnished bronze." Obviously, this is a side of Christ the previous gospels were not shown. One might say that the imagery here reveals Christ in His full glory and authority, ready to deliver righteous judgment. And when we discover the conduct surrounding the church of Thyatira, it's made clear why He would appear this way.

Located in Asia Minor (Turkey), Thyatira was another Roman city marked by immense pagan worship to deities such as Apollo Trimnaeus and Apollo. The city often held guild meetings where meat was sacrificed to guild gods, along with orgies that were conducted together with the meat offerings. And similar to

Pergamum, refusal to participate in the meat fest would lead to rejection from the trade and craft guilds and, ultimately, no way to earn a living.

However, Christ opens with commending words as He did with the previous church by acknowledging their good words, faith, and love for one another. Jesus even says in regard to their works and service that He finds "the last to be more than the first." The church has become more organized over time and is able to feed, house, and teach more people than before.

But despite an increase in good works, they have erred from the teaching of the true gospel. Jesus begins Revelation 2:20 critiquing the church's tolerance of "that woman Jezebel." Here, Christ is speaking of the spiritual influence of the Phoenician wife of the wicked king Ahab in the book of 1 Kings. When she was alive on earth, she used manipulation and persuasion to have her king Ahab commit many evils in Israel. Therefore, godless women with characteristics such as these were dubbed with the name Jezebel.

The spirit of Jezebel was corrupting the church of Thyatira by persuading believers through women in the city to eat meat sacrificed to idols and their guild gods in addition to performing sexually immoral acts. Christ rebukes Jezebel for calling herself a prophetess while committing such heinous acts. In Revelation 2:21, He was even merciful and said that he gave her space to repent of her fornication, but she refused.

Her refusal marked the signing of her death sentence as Christ vowed to throw Jezebel into a sick bed, as well as those who commit adultery with her into great tribulation until they repent of their evil deeds in corrupting His church. Then in verse 23, He says, "I will strike her children dead." By children, Christ is referring to those who follow the teachings of Jezebel.

He continues in verse 23 by declaring that all the church will know that He is the one who searches the hearts and minds of each believer. Therefore, it would be impossible to hide our sin from Him, since each person will be rewarded according to their works.

In verse 24, Christ reassures those who don't subscribe to Jezebel's tactics that they are safe and He will put no other burden on them seeing that Jezebel's wiles are burdensome enough already. The destructive doctrines were even called the deep secrets of Satan because of the havoc they caused.

From Revelation 2:25–29, Christ encourages those who are in the truth to hold fast to the true gospel until He comes. He goes on to give a grand promise to those who overcome the temptations of false teachings that He will give them power over the nations when His Kingdom is fully established on earth. Such believers will share with Him in ruling the nations with a rod of iron as He received the authority from His Father. Those who have spiritual ears to hear are encouraged to listen to how the Spirit is leading the church.

Prophetic Significance of the Thyatira Church

As we're aware, the Romans were known for their ruthless persecution of Christians. Being that it was impossible to eradicate the Christian faith, the church rather married itself to the government. Soon enough, the church became the government and was dominated by the Roman Catholic institution. Being that the church during Thyatira was the ruling political power, conversion was less of faith and more of political necessity.

While they performed great social responsibilities, these works were devoid of the backing of the true gospel of Jesus Christ, thus opening the door for all sorts of heresies, spiritual offenses, and strongholds like Jezebel. Many of these heresies still exist today in the Roman Catholic Church and include the following:

- worship of idols and images
- celibacy of priests (a Nicolaitan practice)
- justification and salvation through works rather than faith alone
- passivity of sin and immoralities
- using a man rather than Christ as a mediator

End-of-Chapter Quiz

1. What do the seven stars and seven lampstands represent in Revelation 2:1?
2. Which church was accused of leaving their first love and why?
3. Which church experienced great poverty because of their faith in Christ?
4. In what church were the teachings of Balaam and the Nicolaitans practiced?
5. Who is Jezebel and in which church did her spirit dwell?

Answers

1. The seven stars represent seven angels, and the seven lampstands point to the seven churches receiving the letters from Jesus.
2. The church of Ephesus was told that they left their first love (Jesus) because their service to God became mundane.
3. The believers in the church of Smyrna were considered criminals and suffered outward poverty for their loyalty to Christ but had eternal blessings in heaven.
4. The church of Pergamum held the doctrine of Balaam and the Nicolaitans, which Christ hated.
5. Jezebel was the Phoenician wife of King Ahab of Israel mentioned in 1 Kings and was regarded as a wicked woman. Her spirit and teachings corrupted the believers in the church of Thyatira.

3

REVELATION 3—THE SEVEN SPIRITS

REVELATION 3:1–22

To the Church in Sardis

To the angel of the church in Sardis write: These are the words of him who holds the seven spirits of God and the seven stars. I know your deeds; you have a reputation of being alive, but you are dead. Wake up! Strengthen what remains and is about to die, for I have found your deeds unfinished in the sight of my God. Remember, therefore, what you have received and heard; hold it fast, and repent. But if you do not wake up, I will come like a thief, and you will not know at what time I will come to you. Yet you have a few people in Sardis who have not soiled their clothes. They will walk with me, dressed in white, for they are worthy. The one who is victorious will, like them, be dressed in white. I will never blot out the name of that person from the book of life, but will acknowledge that name before my Father and his angels. Whoever has ears, let them hear what the Spirit says to the churches.

To the Church in Philadelphia
To the angel of the church in Philadelphia write: These are the words of him who is holy and true, who holds the key of David. What he opens no one can shut, and what he shuts no one can open. I know your deeds. See, I have placed before you an open door that no one can shut. I know that you have little strength, yet you have kept my word and have not denied my name. I will make those who are of the synagogue of Satan, who claim to be Jews though they are not, but are liars—I will make them come and fall down at your feet and acknowledge that I have loved you. Since you have kept my command to endure patiently, I will also keep you from the hour of trial that is going to come on the whole world to test the inhabitants of the earth. I am coming soon. Hold on to what you have, so that no one will take your crown. The one who is victorious I will make a pillar in the temple of my God. Never again will they leave it. I will write on them the name of my God and the name of the city of my God, the new Jerusalem, which is coming down out of heaven from my God; and I will also write on them my new name. Whoever has ears, let them hear what the Spirit says to the churches.

To the Church in Laodicea
To the angel of the church in Laodicea write: These are the words of the Amen, the faithful and true witness, the ruler

> of God's creation. I know your deeds, that you are neither cold nor hot. I wish you were either one or the other! So, because you are lukewarm—neither hot nor cold—I am about to spit you out of my mouth. You say, 'I am rich; I have acquired wealth and do not need a thing.' But you do not realize that you are wretched, pitiful, poor, blind and naked. I counsel you to buy from me gold refined in the fire, so you can become rich; and white clothes to wear, so you can cover your shameful nakedness; and salve to put on your eyes, so you can see. Those whom I love I rebuke and discipline. So be earnest and repent. Here I am! I stand at the door and knock. If anyone hears my voice and opens the door, I will come in and eat with that person, and they with me. To the one who is victorious, I will give the right to sit with me on my throne, just as I was victorious and sat down with my Father on his throne. Whoever has ears, let them hear what the Spirit says to the churches.

Revelation 3:1–6 Revealed

Church of Sardis

Beginning in Revelation 3:1, Jesus describes Himself as He "who holds the seven spirits of God and the seven stars" (angels), alluding to His all-knowing nature. He tells the church of Sardis that although they have a name that they are alive, they are in fact dead. The death He is speaking of is in terms of their deeds. But to better understand why Christ refers to their "name," we must first define what Sardis means.

Located just 60 miles northeast of the city of Smyrna, which was covered in the previous chapter, Sardis was a city of Asia Minor and scholars translated the name to mean "those escaping" or "remnant." That sounds like a church that has a name to live up to! They were undoubtedly successful due to their enormous temples and fertile soil, but their spiritual deeds were lacking according to Christ's standards.

The book of James echoes this same understanding when it says in James 2:17, "In the same way, faith by itself, if it is not accompanied by action, is dead." Having faith in God without having the deeds of a transformed lifestyle is, indeed, a dead faith. It's for this reason that they are instructed by the Lord in verse 2 to strengthen the deeds that are remaining before their faith is completely dead because their works (or deeds) have not been found perfect before God.

- The fact that He says in Revelation 3:2 to "wake up" means there must have been a spirit of apathy or laziness that came over the church, and Christ was giving them a chance to redeem themselves and rediscover the purpose of the church.
- Strengthening what remains means that there were still some believers in the church who were willing to marry their deeds with their faith. This small group of believers is what is called the remnant. Without their presence in the church, their lampstand would be removed.

So not only has the church of Sardis not fulfilled the purpose of Christ in their ministry by deed, but their work is also seen as incomplete in the sight of God the Father. While every believer should prioritize anchoring their faith on the truth of the doctrine, putting that faith into practice through works is still a major requirement to be pleasing to God.

However, that doesn't imply that you should justify the worship of false gods and idols by providing food and shelter to the hungry and homeless. Believers must adhere to the pure doctrine of Christ for the health and salvation of their souls while simultaneously exercising outward expressions of their love for Jesus.

In Revelation 3:3, the remnant is urged to strengthen their resolve by receiving the message of hope and restoration and repenting of their deeds or lack thereof. Christ warns that if they will not watch, repent, and wake up, then He will visit them as a thief when they least expect it. Thieves in the natural world can empty an entire house if the owner is in a deep slumber. Similarly, if the believers will not heed Christ's warning and wake up quickly, they will find that the spirit of God is removed, leaving behind empty churches, empty religious systems, and the vapid lives of believers.

The idea of the remnant who Christ has called to "strengthen the things which remain" is confirmed in verse 4 when He says that there are some in Sardis who have not soiled their garments (with sin) for they walk in white and are worthy.

The color white in the Bible represents purity and salvation, which is further confirmed in Revelation 3:5 which reads, "The one who is victorious will, like them, be dressed in white. I will never blot out the name of that person from the book of life, but will acknowledge that name before my Father and his angels."

When the Bible speaks of putting on garments, it is reserved for believers who have put their faith in Jesus: "For all of you who were baptized into Christ have clothed yourselves with Christ." (Galatians 3:27).

Therefore, for anyone to even have "soiled" garments means they are already believers.

Revelation 3:4–6

Contrary to the purity of white garments, the word "soiled" is literally defined as dirty or stained. So that means that a large majority of the believers in Sardis wore dirty, stained, or blemished spiritual garments. The condition of the believer's walk with Christ would determine how white or how dirty their garments were.

Confirmation of this can also be found later on in the Book of Revelation:

- "Let us rejoice and be glad and give him glory! For the wedding of the Lamb has come, and his bride has made herself ready" (Revelation 19:7).
- "'Fine linen, bright and clean, was given her to wear' (fine linen stands for the righteous acts of God's holy people)" (Revelation 19:8).

Going back to Revelation 3:5, Christ encourages the believers who have overcome and wear white garments that their names will not be blotted out of the Book of Life. In addition, He will also confess their names before His heavenly Father and the angels. It ended in Revelation 3:6 with the usual salutation that whoever has an ear should hear what the spirit of God was communicating.

Prophetic Significance of the Sardis Church

Following the spiritual decadence of the Catholic Church, the church of Sardis lived up to its name as the "called-out" Reformation Church. We mentioned that the name Sardis meant "those escaping" or "remnant," and they were doing just that by escaping the previous apostate church institution.

Many of the heretical beliefs of the Catholic Church were removed which gave birth to the Reformers. During this time, the Lutheran, Anglican, and Presbyterian churches were the dominating faiths, giving rise to the Protestant Church later on.

Revelation 3:7–13 Revealed

Church of Philadelphia

The next church is likely one of the most exemplary of all the churches found in the letters of Revelation—the church of Philadelphia. Founded by King Attalus of Pergamum, also dubbed Philadelphus of Pergamum, the name Philadelphia actually means brotherly love. The city was small but prosperous with the only disadvantage being the frequent earthquakes it suffered.

Due to the frequent pattern of earthquakes, many of the citizens decided to settle in the countryside to avoid the disasters which stunted the growth of the city and the church. However, the uncertainty of those natural disasters taught them perseverance, dependence on, and faith in God.

Jesus introduced Himself in Revelation 3:7 as He who is holy, and true, and has the key of David. He further reminds the church of

His authority by stating that only He has the power to open and shut any doors at will. Holding the key of David refers to the book of Ezekiel which states that in the coming kingdom, David will manage the court of the temple and has the key to the temple. This communicates that Christ is authorized to grant access to the mercy seat in the temple.

The Messiah comforts the church by informing them of an open door that He has set before them that no man can shut. An open door in this context means that there is an opportunity for the church to reach the lost and the enemy can do nothing to stop it. The fact that Christ lets us know that He holds the key of David lets us know that He is fully in control of those opportunities.

He goes on to state in Revelation 3:8 that the Philadelphia church has a little strength, has kept His Word, and has not denied His name. Having little strength refers to the church's size as well as the fact that they knew they were helpless without God, a relationship the earthquakes might've helped to foster. The disasters themselves opened up an opportunity for the gospel to be preached, and so they became a model church for evangelism.

If you noticed, Philadelphia is the only other church beside Smyrna that received no condemnation from the Lord. Both churches were faithful in one way or another to the gospel of Christ despite the persecution they faced which attracted the Lord's love and favor. He makes His love known in Revelation 3:9 by declaring that He would make the false Jews of the synagogue of Satan bow down in reverence to them for His name's sake.

To the average person, it sounds like Christ will deal such a deadly blow to the false Jews that they will be forced to come groveling at their feet for forgiveness. But that's not the way God humbles our enemies in His kingdom. Christ says in 2 Peter 3:9 that he is "not wanting anyone to perish, but everyone to come to repentance." He will use their persecution as a testimony of His love for His people, which will in turn convert the oppressors, causing them to "bow down" in surrender.

He further expresses His love for the Philadelphia church by promising to preserve them from the hour of testing that will come upon the whole world because they have persevered in keeping His Word. Scholars believe this to be talking of the church being spared the persecution brought to the other cities during the reign of the ruthless emperor Domitian from 81 to 96.

However, there was no temptation that befell the whole earth as spoken of in Revelation 3:10. Therefore, we can surmise that this warning is prophetic in nature. The understanding of this worldwide testing will become more clear in the coming chapters of Revelation.

In Revelation 3:11, He alerts His followers that He is coming quickly and that they should hold fast what they have gained so that no one may take their crown. This is a reminder to not give up and endure to the end, for there will surely be a reward at the end of our race of faith.

He concludes the letter to the church of Philadelphia in Revelation 3:12–13 by ensuring believers of their unshakable eternity in the kingdom of God by informing that He will make them into pillars in God's temple. The imagery of being made a pillar in God's temple is in contrast to the unstable, earthquake-prone city of Philadelphia that caused many of the citizens to flee to the countryside outside of the city for shelter.

With the church of Philadelphia set apart as a witness of the true gospel of Jesus Christ, there was still one more church that needed to be addressed. Prophetically, this church would mark the end of the church age and is a prime example of the current state of Christ's church today.

Revelation 3:14–22 Revealed

Church of Laodicea

Probably the most dreaded word in the Book of Revelation to any true believer is "lukewarm." And that's exactly the description Christ uses for this next church, the church of Laodicea. This church was not only a prosperous commercial and administrative center, but it was actually the richest city in the Roman Empire. Laodicea was so wealthy that it refused to accept Imperial aid to rebuild the city, opting to fund the cost themselves and remain independent from Roman authority. But as you'll learn in a few verses, this immense wealth is exactly the reason they are served with a soul-crushing rebuke from the Lord.

Christ begins by describing Himself as "the Amen, the faithful and true witness, the ruler of God's creation" (Revelation 3:14). He then jumps straight into their deeds, informing them that He knows that they are neither hot nor cold. This is a direct reflection of their faith in the sight of Jesus. It is meant to imply that they are neither fervent in their faith nor are they completely reprobate—they are lukewarm. Being lukewarm is essentially being on the fence.

- A lukewarm Christian is one who is not fully committed to the things of God but still identifies themselves as

believers. So although Christ may be on their lips, they prove by their deeds that He is far from their hearts.
- This sort of believer lacks a solid foundation and is often unstable and double minded.

Jesus says in verse 15 that He wished they were either hot or cold—either for Him or against Him. As a result of their lukewarm state, He says that He will spew them out of His mouth. The literal translation of His words means that He will "vomit" them out of His mouth, which is quite a graphic depiction of rejection but lets us know how disgusted He is with their behavior.

In verse 17, they are admonished for being rich and believing that they lack nothing, indicating their delusional state. But Christ brings them back down to earth by informing them of their true state—wretched, miserable, poor, blind, and naked. Of course, the believers in Laodicea did not walk around physically naked, but spiritually, the covering of Christ was missing. In essence, you can see that on an earthly level, the church of Laodicea was wealthy, but they were spiritually impoverished.

As a result, Christ provides some remedies to cure their spiritual plight:

- In Revelation 3:18, He counsels them to buy gold tried in the fire so they can be made rich. Gold refined by fire is a common analogy in the Scripture used to define the eternal treasures of our deeds in Christ. This is meant to aid their spiritual poverty.
- He includes white raiment to the list so that "you can cover your shameful nakedness." We discussed what white

raiment means in the letter to the church of Sardis that it signifies purity, salvation, and being clothed with Christ.

- They are also instructed to anoint their eyes with eye salve so they can see, as a means of curing their spiritual blindness. This means that they are lacking a knowledge of God's truth.

They are also reminded in verse 19 that all of this correction and admonition is out of love. Christ says, "Those whom I love I rebuke and discipline. So be earnest and repent." Like any good parent who loves their children enough to discipline them, God does the same with us as believers. And it's all to cause us to repent. We can surmise that a life of too much ease and luxury could be the death of a believer's faith if they neglect the more important spiritual riches like training and conviction.

In Revelation 3:20–22, Jesus reminds us that He stands at the door (of a believer's heart) and knocks. Being the gentleman He is, Christ always nudges us instead of forcefully demanding us to be converted. He goes on to say that if anyone hears His voice and invites Him in (to their hearts), He will sup with them and provide the spiritual food they have been missing.

Again, in verse 21, He offers those who overcome to sit with Him in His throne and rule, even as He sat on His Father's throne after He overcame.

As always, the letter concludes by encouraging those who have spiritual ears to hear and understand what His Spirit is saying to the churches.

End-of-Chapter Quiz

1. What did Jesus mean when He said the church of Sardis had a name of being alive, and what does the name Sardis mean?
2. Why did Christ say the church of Sardis was dead?
3. Which church in this chapter doesn't receive a condemnation from God?
4. What natural disaster often strikes the church of Philadelphia?
5. What is the biggest flaw of the Laodicean Church?

Answers

1. The word "Sardis" means remnant. The word remnant means the small remainder of a quantity of something. In biblical terms, a remnant is a called-out group of people that serve God faithfully.
2. Despite having the name of being a "remnant" church, there are no works to match their faith. And faith without works is dead.
3. The church of Philadelphia is one of two churches that does not receive the Lord's rebuke.
4. The church of Philadelphia often suffered from earthquakes.
5. The church of Laodicea was rebuked by Jesus for being lukewarm, meaning they were not completely committed to the Christian faith.

4

REVELATION 4—THE THRONE ROOM OF HEAVEN

REVELATION 4:1–11

The Throne in Heaven

After this I looked, and there before me was a door standing open in heaven. And the voice I had first heard speaking to me like a trumpet said, "Come up here, and I will show you what must take place after this." At once I was in the Spirit, and there before me was a throne in heaven with someone sitting on it. And the one who sat there had the appearance of jasper and sardius. A rainbow that shone like an emerald encircled the throne. Surrounding the throne were twenty-four other thrones, and seated on them were twenty-four elders. They were dressed in white and had crowns of gold on their heads. From the throne came flashes of lightning, rumblings and peals of thunder. In front of the throne, seven lamps were blazing. These are the seven spirits of God.

> Also in front of the throne there was what looked like a sea of glass, clear as crystal. In the center, around the throne, were four living creatures, and they were covered with eyes, in front and in back. The first living creature was like a lion, the second was like an ox, the third had a face like a man, the fourth was like a flying eagle. Each of the four living creatures had six wings and was covered with eyes all around, even under its wings. Day and night they never stop saying: "'Holy, holy, holy is the Lord God Almighty,' who was, and is, and is to come." Whenever the living creatures give glory, honor and thanks to him who sits on the throne and who lives for ever and ever, the twenty-four elders fall down before him who sits on the throne and worship him who lives for ever and ever. They lay their crowns before the throne and say: "You are worthy, our Lord and God, to receive glory and honor and power, for you created all things, and by your will they were created and have their being."

Daniel 2:1–16 Revealed

As we've discussed earlier, the sequence in which Jesus instructed John to write the Book of Revelation was in three parts, consisting of things in the past tense, present tense, and future tense. And if one is to study the Bible in depth, you will see that there are many prophetic books in the Old Testament that point to the future, more specifically, the Book of Revelation. And even in the Book of Revelation, some of the letters that John wrote were not even for his time, but for the church of the last days, which we are currently living in.

There are certain prophetic books of the Bible written specifically for the "last days" or the "end of the age." Therefore, to better understand the timeline of the Book of Revelation, we'll need to consider previous books of the Bible that coincide with the "last days" of Revelation.

It's also important to understand the concept of ages, especially surrounding the topic of the last days and prophecy.

- Ages are defined as a lengthy but determinate time period in God's historical schedule.
- Ages follow each other in a continuous sequence, and each division between ages serve as important demarcations in God's program.

So it can therefore be established that the "last days" we are living in are merely the end of a certain age, and once it ends, it will signal the beginning of the next age, which we will uncover. With all this talk of ages, times, and seasons, your next question might be, "What age are we living in?"

Christ gives us the answer in Luke 21:24, "They will fall by the sword and will be taken as prisoners to all the nations. Jerusalem will be trampled on by the Gentiles until the times of the Gentiles are fulfilled."

Jesus lets us know in this passage that we are in the "age of the Gentiles." The word Gentile in the Scripture refers to all non-Jews, meaning that we are currently in the time when Gentiles have more power on earth than Israel.

With that said, we'll begin by going back to the Book of Daniel to better understand the events that led to the Gentiles gaining power over Israel. We'll be looking specifically at Daniel 2:1–16 and Daniel 2:24–45 as well as Daniel 7 as they both explain the age of the Gentiles.

The second chapter of Daniel begins by introducing us to King Nebuchadnezzar who reigned over the province of Babylon. His name stands out in Bible history because it was under his directive that Babylon invaded the southern kingdom of Judah and captured Jerusalem in 597 B.C.E. This would be the first time the city fell at the hands of a foreign enemy since King David established Jerusalem as the Jewish capital.

As was the custom of rival kingdoms, King Nebuchadnezzar took captives from Judah as slaves into Babylon. Daniel was among those captured, and he was used by God mightily, bringing glory to God's name even within the walls of their enemies.

The main reason this is accomplished is because of a disturbing dream Nebuchadnezzar received during his second year as king. The Chaldeans, magicians, and sorcerers were unable to interpret the dream for him and thought that there was not a man on earth who could do it. Daniel is given access to supernatural wisdom from God and is able to solve the riddle the king made and interpret the dream.

Daniel 2:25–45

King Nebuchadnezzar became so upset that the magicians and sorcerers could not interpret his dream that he ordered all the wise men of Babylon to be killed, which included Daniel and his friends. But Daniel wisely inquires of Arioch, the king's commander, the reason the decree was sent forth. When Arioch explains the matter, Daniel agrees to give the interpretation but requests time to receive it from God.

In Daniel 2:25, Daniel, who is given the name Belteshazzar, is rushed to the presence of King Nebuchadnezzar as he is the only one among the exiles from Judah who has his interpretation. Daniel reminds the king that there was no power in the magicians and sorcerers to reveal the interpretation of his dream. He says in Daniel 2:28 that "there is a God in heaven who reveals mysteries. He has shown King Nebuchadnezzar what will happen in days to come."

If you jump to Daniel 2:31, the prophet Daniel details Nebuchadnezzar's dream beginning with the figure of a huge statue: the head made of fine gold, its breast and arms made of silver, its belly and thighs of bronze, its legs of iron, and its feet mixed with iron and clay. He continued to explain that a stone struck the statue on its feet and crushed them. Later in verse 35, he confirms that this same stone grew into a great mountain that covered the earth.

Skip down to Daniel 2:37–38, and you'll see that Daniel attributes the statue's head of gold to King Nebuchadnezzar and his kingdom of Babylon as the ruler over the body of the statue. He also let it be known to the Babylonian king that it is Daniel's God, the God of heaven, who has given the kingdoms making up the statue into his hand. Essentially, only by God's decree is Nebuchadnezzar able to rule over every earthly kingdom.

Daniel confirms this in verse 44 when he says:

> In the time of those kings, the God of heaven will set up a kingdom that will never be destroyed, nor will it be left to

> another people. It will crush all those kingdoms and bring them to an end, but it will itself endure forever.

It is understood by Daniel's interpretation that Nebuchadnezzar, king of Babylon, was given the authority by God to rule over every portion of the earth for an assigned time. That means that Nebuchadnezzar's reigns and Babylon's dominance, or the "age of the Gentiles," would eventually come to an end.

Not only do the different body parts and metals represent various kingdoms, but they also represent a timeline in history, specifically for our age, which was and still is being ruled by the Gentiles, until the stone that "was cut out without hands" strikes the feet of the statue. And since this stone represents the age of the Gentiles and the kingdoms of man, the stone that crushes the statue's feet represents a new kingdom being set up to replace the former. This new kingdom will be more powerful than any of the former kingdoms of gold, silver, bronze, or brass; it will be the kingdom of Christ on earth. Let's briefly identify each earthly kingdom:

- As we've stated earlier, the head of gold on the statue points to the kingdom of Babylon where Nebuchadnezzar ruled, which also marked the beginning of the age of the Gentiles.
- The second kingdom is of silver and represents that of the Medo-Persians, which was formed through an alliance between the Medes and Persians and replaced the kingdom of Babylon in 550 B.C.E. It is depicted as silver because it is lesser in power than Nebuchadnezzar's Babylonian kingdom.

- The third kingdom assumes world power but is still of lesser quality than the previous kingdom and is represented as bronze. This is recognized as the Greek Empire and primarily depicted the Hellenistic Empire of Alexander the Great, which came into power in 330 B.C.E.
- The fourth kingdom represents the feet and toes of the statue, signaling the end of the age of the Gentiles. They are depicted as a mixture of iron and clay. Iron is of even lesser value than bronze, and clay is merely dirt, meaning that the last kingdom will be unstable. The kingdom that best depicts this one is the Roman Empire, since it was never completely replaced.

Daniel 7:2–27 Revealed

Daniel said in Chapter 7 verses 2–6:

> In my vision at night I looked, and there before me were the four winds of heaven churning up the great sea. Four great beasts, each different from the others, came up out of the sea. The first was like a lion, and it had the wings of an eagle. I watched until its wings were torn off and it was lifted from the ground so that it stood on two feet like a human being, and the mind of a human was given to it. And there before me was a second beast, which looked like a bear. It was raised up on one of its sides, and it had three ribs in its mouth between its teeth. It was told, 'Get up and eat your fill of flesh!' After that, I looked, and there before me was another beast, one that looked like a leopard. And on its back it had four wings like those of a bird.

> This beast had four heads, and it was given authority to rule.

Daniel 7 goes into even further detail about the kingdoms that will rule during the age of the Gentiles. The number of animals mentioned are four, which lines up perfectly with the above text scripture for Daniel 2 and the statue of gold, silver, bronze, and clay.

Beginning in Daniel 7:2–6, Daniel is the one who now receives a vision of four winds stirring up the sea. He then sees four great beasts, all different in feature, coming up from the sea:

- The first was like unto a lion with the wings of an eagle that appeared to be missing, which synchronizes with the gold head of Nebuchadnezzar's Babylonian kingdom. The lion was also made to stand on two feet like a man and had the mind of a man, which again parallels Nebuchadnezzar.
- The second beast resembled a lopsided bear with three ribs in its mouth, and it was told to "get up and eat your fill of flesh!" The bear represents the Medo-Persians and reached peak power by conquering Lydia, Babylonia, and Egypt, hence the three ribs in its mouth.
- The third kingdom is described as the third animal—a four-headed leopard with four wings on its back. This would, of course, represent the third kingdom, which is the Greek Empire. The Greeks expanded their empire swiftly and speedily in a short matter of time.

Now, Daniel begins to describe the fourth kingdom in Daniel 7:7 and wasn't even able to find a suitable animal to compare it to because it was so monstrous. He describes the fourth beast as "terrifying and frightening and very powerful. It had large iron teeth." He goes on to say that "it was different from all the former beasts, and it had ten horns." Daniel details that he saw a little horn come up among the other horns which had eyes like the eyes of a man and a mouth uttering great things.

There is an undeniable similarity between the first and last kingdoms, as they both seem to be ruled by an individual man. The little horn, which is the 11th horn on the head of the beast, is the most ruthless because it uproots three of the ten horns and assumes its place as the leader of the remaining horns. Many believe this to be the Antichrist spoken of in the Book of Revelation. It should be known that the horns on the fourth beast that are mentioned are world leaders on the political stage in one way or the other.

Daniel 7:9–10

Then in verse 9, Daniel sees a vision of the Lord in the throne room which correlates with what John saw in Revelation 4:1. He also sees thrones and the Ancient of Days (Jesus Christ) taking His seat on one of the thrones. Christ is described as being dressed in a garment as white as snow (white again alluding to His purity, divinity, and light) with a head of hair like pure wool. His depiction is similar to Revelation 1:14 which also describes Christ with hair as white as wool. Daniel then confirms that God's throne is ablaze with flames, perhaps the seven spirits of God mentioned in Revelation 1:5.

In verse 10, Daniel tells of a river of fire flowing from before His throne as well as thousands upon thousands of angels that were standing before Him. A very similar image is explained in Revelation 4:8. We are given a sneak preview of what the everlasting kingdom of

Christ will look like once the time of the Gentiles has come to an irredeemable end.

Revelation 4:1–6 Revealed

Now that we have laid some foundational work regarding when and how the age of the Gentiles began, we can now return to Revelation 4. The previous chapter highlighted the seven letters to the church and points to the fact that we are still in the church age because the body of Christ is still on earth. However, the church is presently living during the age of the Gentiles, which we thoroughly discussed previously.

Revelation 4 gives us a brief depiction of what the Lord's throne will look like. John details in Revelation 4:2 that while he was in the Spirit, he witnessed a throne in heaven with someone sitting on it whose appearance was bright and magnificent as a jasper or a ruby. The word jasper is actually an ancient term for diamond, and sardius is a fiery red gem, giving us an idea of how luminous and dazzling God's throne is. He also recalled seeing a rainbow surround the throne. Not only does the rainbow add to the aesthetic of the scene, but rainbows in the Bible denote the glory and promises of God, as we find in Genesis 9:13, "I have set my rainbow in the clouds, and it will be the sign of the covenant between me and the earth."

Besides the main throne which is presumably occupied by Jesus, Revelation 4:4 gives further detail to 24 other thrones surrounding it which are occupied by 24 elders who are all dressed in white with gold crowns on their heads. When the word elder is mentioned in the Bible, it doesn't necessarily mean someone who is old but rather figures who lead God's people. And the fact that they are given their own thrones signifies their position of authority to reign alongside Jesus.

From Revelation 4:1, it appears that John is shown an open door in heaven and again hears a voice like the sound of a trumpet, much like the one he heard in Revelation 1:10, so we know it's Jesus' voice who is calling him to show him "what must take place after this." In keeping with the context, it seems that Jesus is speaking of events that must unfold after the church age since it comes directly after the seven letters to the church.

In Revelation 4:5, we see that the throne is decorated with flashes of lightning and peals of thunder, which is another testament to God's power and glory. The seven spirits of God also appear in front of the throne as burning lamps. The imagery of a burning lamp is representative of the presence of the spirit of God, as He has taken on other forms such as a dove.

Revelation 4:7–11 Revealed

John also sees four otherworldly creatures who some scholars believe to be seraphim angels. Revelation 4:8 tells us that the four living creatures are covered with eyes all over their body and never stop praising, saying, "'Holy, holy, holy is the Lord God Almighty,' who was, and is, and is to come." We are told that the 24 elders also fall down and worship the one who sits on the throne, laying their crowns before the throne in reverence.

The Greek word John uses for crown is *stephanos*, which is typically described as an award for excellent performance for a particular task or field of expertise. The same Greek word is used to describe the wreath given to competing athletes in the Greek Olympic Games. Only as believers, when we run the race of faith set before us and finish it, our crown is eternal life, as stated in 2 Timothy 4:7–8:

> I have fought the good fight, I have finished the race, I have kept the faith. Now there is in store for me the crown of righteousness, which the Lord, the righteous Judge, will award to me on that day—and not only to me, but also to all who have longed for his appearing.

This is also an indication that in heaven, there is no end to the worship and praise for God and His magnificent power. The angels are known for exalting God as worthy of honor, power, and endless glory. We will find that there are angels in heaven whose job is to serve the Father on His throne with nonstop praise and worship.

We are also given an idea of the atmosphere of praise in heaven in Revelation 4:9–11. It states that when the angelic creatures give honor and glory to the one on the throne, the elders also join in, signaling that giving praise and adoration to God is the lifestyle and language of heaven.

End-of-Chapter Quiz

1. When did the age of the Gentiles begin?
2. What did King Nebuchadnezzar's dream of the statue represent?
3. Which portion of the Scripture in Daniel's book correlates to John's vision of the throne room of heaven?

4. How many spirits of God are before the throne?
5. How many elders are present before God's throne?

Answers

1. The age of the Gentiles began around 597 B.C.E. when King Nebuchadnezzar, king of Babylon, captured Jerusalem.
2. Daniel's interpretation by way of God's spirit explained that the dream of the statue represents the many kingdoms that will reign over Israel during the age of the Gentiles, beginning with Babylon.
3. Daniel 7:2–27 gives a similar account of John's vision in Revelation 4.
4. There are seven spirits of God before the throne.
5. There are 24 elders before the throne of God.

5

REVELATION 5—THE LAMB TAKES THE SCROLL, WORTHY IS THE LAMB

REVELATION 5:1–14

The Scroll and the Lamb

Then I saw in the right hand of him who sat on the throne a scroll with writing on both sides and sealed with seven seals. And I saw a mighty angel proclaiming in a loud voice, "Who is worthy to break the seals and open the scroll?" But no one in heaven or on earth or under the earth could open the scroll or even look inside it. I wept and wept because no one was found who was worthy to open the scroll or look inside. Then one of the elders said to me, "Do not weep! See, the Lion of the tribe of Judah, the Root of David, has triumphed. He is able to open the scroll and its seven seals." Then I saw a Lamb, looking as if it had been slain, standing at the center of the throne, encircled by the four living creatures and the elders. The Lamb had seven horns and seven

> eyes, which are the seven spirits of God sent out into all the earth. He went and took the scroll from the right hand of him who sat on the throne. And when he had taken it, the four living creatures and the twenty-four elders fell down before the Lamb. Each one had a harp and they were holding golden bowls full of incense, which are the prayers of God's people. And they sang a new song, saying: "You are worthy to take the scroll and to open its seals, because you were slain, and with your blood you purchased for God persons from every tribe and language and people and nation. You have made them to be a kingdom and priests to serve our God, and they will reign on the earth." Then I looked and heard the voice of many angels, numbering thousands upon thousands, and ten thousand times ten thousand. They encircled the throne and the living creatures and the elders. In a loud voice they were saying: "Worthy is the Lamb, who was slain, to receive power and wealth and wisdom and strength and honor and glory and praise!" Then I heard every creature in heaven and on earth and under the earth and on the sea, and all that is in them, saying: "To him who sits on the throne and to the Lamb be praise and honor and glory and power, for ever and ever!" The four living creatures said, "Amen," and the elders fell down and worshiped.

Preview to Revelation 5

To better understand Revelation 5, we'll first need to expound on Revelation 4:5–8 a bit more in depth. The four living, otherworldly creatures mentioned around the throne of God are the highest class of angelic being known as cherubim. Cherubim are guardians of the glory of God, hence the reason they don't seem to cease giving God praise, saying in Revelation 4:8, "'Holy, holy, holy is the Lord God Almighty,' who was, and is, and is to come."

The last place in the Bible where the cherubim were mentioned was in Ezekiel 10 when the guardians of the glory arrived in Jerusalem to escort the glory of God out of His temple ahead of the Babylonian attack, the same attack which has led to the capture of Israel and the age of the Gentiles. The departure of God's glory from the temple meant that His presence has not dwelled among the children of Israel from that time, with Jesus' ministry on earth being an exception.

It's for this reason that the cherubim are at God's side guarding His glory day and night. So in the same way that they were mentioned in Ezekiel 10 to highlight the departure of God's glory from the temple before the Babylonian armies arrived, the mention of them in Revelation 4:6–8 foreshadows the return of God's glory to His temple to dwell among Israel and the earth by extension.

However, before the glory of God can return to earth, there will be many historical events and much wrath that will take place in heaven and on earth. Revelation 5 begins to highlight that time of God's wrath as well as the final seven years of the age of the Gentiles.

Revelation 5 Revealed

Picking up from where John left off in the throne room in Chapter 4, he continues to detail his vision in Chapter 5 of the Father sitting on the throne with a book in His right hand that was sealed with seven seals. The word used for book in this passage is the Greek word *biblion*, which had the appearance of a scroll or a rolled-up document. Important parchments, like legal documents for example, were usually sealed shut with wax seals where the edge of the scroll ends.

However, this particular scroll was sealed with seven seals, reminding us again of the lucky number seven which, as we know, means 100% or completion. Therefore, this is a complete sealing of the scroll. And as we are told in Revelation 5:3–4, its contents remained concealed because there was no one found worthy to open the book (scroll) or look into it.

We can be sure that Father God is the one on the throne because after the angel asks in Revelation 5:2, "Who is worthy to break the seals and open the scroll?" we are introduced to "the Lion of the tribe of Judah, the Root of David, (who) has triumphed. He is able to open the scroll and its seven seals." This is undoubtedly a description of Jesus. But to eliminate any doubt, Revelation 5:6 mentions a lamb standing as if it had been slain between the throne and the elders, having "seven horns and seven eyes, which are the seven spirits of God sent out into all the earth."

John gives an idea of what type of scroll it was by stating that there was writing on both sides (Revelation 5:1). One of the legal documents that most commonly employed this type of wax-sealed presentation were land deeds for the sale or use of land. The content of the deeds detailing the terms for the purchase or use of the land was written inside the document, rolled into a scroll, and sealed. In addition, a summary of the terms of the deed was written on the outside of the scroll informing others of what was agreed to.

But the custom for the transfer of property within Israel was temporary, and the law required the land to return to its rightful owner at the Jubilee year. The seals of the document could only be broken by a magistrate if there were doubts or concerns over the authenticity of the summary. In the event that the seals were broken on the deed, it was declared finished and brought to an end, leading to the formation of a new agreement.

Now, based on John's description, we can rest assured that he has indeed described a land deed. And being that the main topic of discussion has been surrounding Israelites' captivity in Babylon, the land in question would be Israel itself. So from the moment Israel was displaced from their land in 605 B.C.E. and given over to Gentile rule (age of the Gentiles), they have been dominant over Israel for the past 2,600 years.

"See, the Lion of the tribe of Judah, the Root of David, has triumphed" (Revelation 5:5).

But as we mentioned previously that the land is returned to its legal owner every Jubilee year, or 70 years, God has promised that Israel will once again receive their land. If you remember, we also mentioned that only a local leader with authority over the specified land in Israel could break the seal of the land deed. And who would be more able to end the age of Gentiles and restore the land of Israel to its rightful owners?

This is why the question was asked in verse 2, "Who is worthy to break the seals and open the scroll?" Although the Father in heaven is more than worthy to do so, He would be going against His word since He handed Israel's land over to the Gentiles in the first place. This is where Jesus comes in. Someone else would have to be authorized to be an impartial judge of the agreement God has set in place, becoming a mediator in the matter. And who better to do so than the resurrected Lamb of God?

In Revelation 5:7, John sees the slain, resurrected Lamb take the scroll out of the hand of He who sat on the throne. In the previous verse, the Lamb (Jesus Christ) is depicted with seven horns and seven eyes, which are the seven spirits of God, making Him the perfect candidate to break the seven seals on the scroll. The imagery of the seven horns and seven eyes means that He is all-ruling and all-seeing. Jesus has overcome the world and the devil, meaning that His resurrection has given Him rulership over the devil and dominion over the world.

In verses 8–10, the cherubim and the 24 elders erupt into a song of praise while holding golden bowls full of incense, which are the prayers of the saints. The prayers of the saints actually become a form of worship, which is why the cherubim and the elders offer it up with their own song of praise. The song highlights a few important aspects of Christ reclaiming authority over the world based on His death and resurrection:

- His shed blood has purchased people of all nations and tongues.
- Collectively, they have been made into a kingdom of priests unto God.

The Final Scene: Revelation 5:11–14

John's view then switches to reveal an innumerable multitude of angels that surround the throne, the living creatures, and the elders to join in the praise confirming that the Lamb is worthy to inherit the rulership of His kingdom. The announcement of Christ's coming into rulership of His kingdom is so universally significant that every creature in heaven, on earth, under the earth, and under the sea ascribes praise, honor, glory, and power to Him. Even dead unbelievers in hell have to acknowledge Jesus' ascent to the throne.

As the final seven years of Daniel's 70 sevens, or 490 years, approaches, the worst period in the history of the age of the Gentiles since the time of Nebuchadnezzar is preparing to strike. This period is known as the day of the Lord or the seven-year tribulation.

Now that we've dissected the story behind the scroll with seven seals, its correlation to how land deeds and the sale of land was conducted in the Old Testament in Israel, and how it ties in with Jesus being the mediator chosen to restore Israel back to its owners while bringing the age of the Gentiles to a cataclysmic close, we'll be going in to the breaking of the for six of the seven seals. Truly exciting times to be alive!

Going into Revelation Chapter 6, we'll be investigating the start of the tribulation period and the breaking of the seals.

End-of-Chapter Quiz

1. What is the highest angelic rank and what is their duty?
2. Besides the book of Revelation, when was the last time the cherubim were mentioned?
3. What does the number seven mean in the Bible?
4. How is Jesus depicted before God's throne in this picture?

5. Why was Jesus found worthy to break the seven seals and open the scroll?

Answers

1. Cherubims are the highest-ranking angels in heaven and are the guardians of the glory of God.
2. The cherubim were last mentioned in the book of Ezekiel.
3. The number seven means perfection, completion, or 100%.
4. Jesus is depicted as a slain lamb with seven horns and seven eyes, which are the seven spirits of God.
5. Jesus was found worthy because He was slain and His blood was shed to purchase the Israelites back from the Gentiles who captured them.

6

REVELATION 6—THE SIX OF SEVEN SEALS

REVELATION 6:1–17

I watched as the Lamb opened the first of the seven seals. Then I heard one of the four living creatures say in a voice like thunder, "Come!" I looked, and there before me was a white horse! Its rider held a bow, and he was given a crown, and he rode out as a conqueror bent on conquest. When the Lamb opened the second seal, I heard the second living creature say, "Come!" Then another horse came out, a fiery red one. Its rider was given power to take peace from the earth and to make people kill each other. To him was given a large sword. When the Lamb opened the third seal, I heard the third living creature say, "Come!" I looked, and there before me was a black horse! Its rider was holding a pair of scales in his hand. Then I heard what sounded like a voice among the four living creatures, saying, “Two pounds of wheat for a day’s wages, and six pounds of barley for a day’s wages, and do not damage the oil and the wine!” When the Lamb opened the fourth seal, I heard the voice of the fourth living creature say, “Come!” I looked, and there before me was a pale horse! Its rider was named Death, and Hades was following close behind him. They were given power over a fourth of the earth to kill by sword, famine and plague, and by the wild beasts of the earth. When he opened the fifth seal, I saw under the altar the souls of those who had been slain because of the word of God and the testimony they had maintained. They called out in a loud voice, “How long, Sovereign Lord, holy and true, until you judge the inhabitants of the earth and avenge our blood?” Then each of them was given a white robe, and they were told to wait a little longer, until the full number of their fellow servants, their brothers and sisters, were killed just as they had been. I watched as he opened the sixth seal. There was a great earthquake. The sun turned black like sackcloth made of goat hair, the whole moon turned blood red, and the stars in the sky fell to earth, as figs drop from a fig tree when shaken by a strong wind. The heavens receded like a scroll being rolled up, and every mountain and island was removed from its place. Then the kings of the earth, the princes, the generals, the rich, the mighty, and everyone else, both slave and free, hid in caves and among the rocks of the mountains. They called to the mountains and the rocks, “Fall on us and hide us from the face of him who sits on the throne and from the wrath of the Lamb! For the great day of their wrath has come, and who can withstand it?”

Revelation 6 Revealed

There are many signs pointing to the end of the age that are listed in different parts of the Bible, but all coincide with each other. One of the most popular scriptures detailing the events for the end of the age is found in Matthew 24:7–8 which reads: "Nation will rise against nation, and kingdom against kingdom. There will be famines and earthquakes in various places. All these are the beginning of birth pains."

If any of you reading this have experienced childbirth or if you're a man and have a wife who has gone through the pains of labor, then you have some idea of what birth pangs are and why Christ chose to use this analogy to describe the signs of the end.

- Birth pangs, medically recognized as contractions, are mild to intensely painful experiences that a woman goes through during pre-labor. These contractions can gravely interrupt the lives of expecting mothers once they begin. In the same way, the signs of the end of the age will cause many disturbances in the world, and it won't always be business as usual.
- They can sometimes be so mild that they go unnoticed. Some women even mistake their birth pangs as a false alarm due to how unassuming they appear. Similarly, the signs of the end of the age will begin mildly and will go over the heads of many people.
- As it is with preterm labor, no matter how mildly the contractions start, they always increase in intensity and

within closer intervals as time progresses. The frequent repetition and closeness of the contractions signifies that the birth is soon approaching. This is mirrored in the closeness, severity, and frequency of the signs of the times that the end is approaching.
- Birth pangs in pregnancy are a sign pointing to the soon birth of a new life. The birth pangs felt during the end of the age are signs pointing to the end of the world, the anticipated return of Christ and the birthing of His kingdom on earth. This includes a brand-new heaven and earth for Israel and all believers.

Christ also warns of an increase in wars, famines, and earthquakes as additional signposts of His coming. One only has to look back at history to see the transformative effects of WWI and WWII, not to mention the current wars being fought throughout the decades since then. These wars have progressively intensified over the decades, becoming more detrimental as years go by.

The same can be said for famines and earthquakes—each increases in intensity in various parts of the world. Climatologists and world governments put the blame on climate change, but true believers know and understand that these events are all part of the birth pangs.

While the turning over of Israel to the Gentiles marked the beginning of the age of the Gentiles, the signing of a peace deal with Israel and the man of sin, as mentioned in the Book of Daniel 9. According to Verse by Verse Ministry International (2019e), the tribulation spoken of in Revelation can be broken down into three parts:

- the first half of tribulation (Chapters 6–9)
- the mid-tribulation (Chapters 10–15)
- the great tribulation (Chapters 16–19)

So we'll start by uncovering the first half of the tribulation beginning with Revelation 6:1–2.

The Breaking of the Six Seals

The First Seal

We left off in Chapter 5 with Jesus taking the seven seals scroll, making Him the holder of the land deed for earth. As He breaks open the first seal, John is told to "come" by one of the four living creatures. His attention is then drawn to a vision on earth where he first sees a rider perched on a white horse with a bow in his hand. The text goes on to say that a crown was given to him and went out to conquer. But the rider isn't given an identity.

Bible scholars believe this to be the Antichrist since the word "crown" in Revelation 6:2 is the Greek word *stephanos,* which means a crown that is earned in recognition of achievements. This suggests that the mystery rider is either a political or military power, and that possibility is reinforced by the fact that he rides a white horse, which is also the traditional riding style of a military commander.

Remember, the rider on the white horse is going forth "conquering and to conquer," meaning that he is likely motivated by conquering the entire world.

It is also known as the seed of the serpent or the Antichrist who will be solely responsible for starting the tribulation once he signs the peace covenant in the Middle East. In reality, this "peace covenant" will bring the opposite of peace, because he is the father of lies and the embodiment of Satan. That's precisely why he is connected to the first seal, because without his blasphemous actions, the wrath of God would not take place.

The Second Seal

The next horse to be released after Jesus breaks the second seal is the fiery red horse. Revelation 6:3–4 reveals the nature of the rider of this horse, stating that he "was given power to take peace from the earth and to make people kill each other." Here, we find that just as the color of this horse is red, its rider was given the power to bring bloodshed to earth while also removing peace from it.

But we find that just as the rider on the white horse held a bow in his hand, the rider on the red horse is also carrying an object—this time a sword. The fact that he was given power to take peace from earth and cause people to kill each other sounds like the effects of war.

But some may be wondering what the identity of this red horse rider is, since we've concluded that the rider on the white horse is the Antichrist. And the answer is simple; it's also the Antichrist. In the first seal, he appeared on the world stage wearing a crown like a king with the intent to conquer. In the second seal, he plans to conquer through death, carnage, and destruction.

For those who can remember how destructive WWII was, we can only expect greater intensity with WWIII that the Antichrist provokes as he is motivated by worldwide conquest.

The Third Seal

Jesus proceeds to open the third seal which unleashes a different color horse and rider that causes a new wave of calamity on earth—the black horse. Revelation 6:5–6 tells us that the rider of the black horse had a pair of scales in his hand. Scales are generally used to symbolize justice, but in ancient times, scales were used to determine or compare the value of an item for sale. Different objects were placed on either side of the scale, and once they balanced out, their value was said to be equal.

Scales were also used to weigh coin money when it was used to ensure the correct amount of precious metal was being paid. Thus, the scales being held by the black horse rider (the Antichrist) is meant to communicate the negative economic impact he will have in the world, specifically in retail commerce.

So far, we are given the strategy of the Antichrist to "go forth and conquer." He first makes his appearance bearing a bow after the first seal is broken, showing that he has intent to make war. Then, with the release of the red horse, he is given authority to make war and cause bloodshed. History has taught us that what follows after war is usually a devastating economic crisis, which is what the scales in the hands of the black horse rider represents.

In Revelation 6:6, John hears a voice among one of the four living creatures saying, "Two pounds of wheat for a day's wages, and six pounds of barley for a day's wages, and do not damage the oil and the wine!" This is a direct reflection of the hyperinflation that will be caused by the war initiated by the Antichrist.

The Fourth Seal

With the fourth seal now being broken by the Lamb, it releases a pale horse. Revelation 6:8 says, "I looked, and there before me was a pale horse! Its rider was named Death, and Hades was following close behind him."

Following the red horse of bloodshed and the black horse of economic downturn, it only makes sense that death would follow close behind.

Most of us are familiar with the scripture in John 10:10 which reads: "The thief comes only to steal and kill and destroy."

This is exactly what the Antichrist has accomplished through his depiction through the first four seals. The fact that the rider's name is death and he has Hades following close behind him indicates that the Antichrist's ultimate plan is to spread death on earth. Since Hades is a name given to a place called hell, the enemy wants to kill and snatch as many souls to hell as possible.

The pale horse is so powerful that we're told in verse 8 it kills one fourth of mankind on earth by sword, famine, plague, and the wild beasts of the earth.

The Fifth Seal

The opening of the fifth seal gives us a break from the horseman release. Instead of being on earth, John's focus is drawn once again to the scene in heaven where he sees the altar. The altar is a significant place because it is the place where sacrifices are offered up to God. Revelation 6:9 lets us know that the sacrifices under the altar were the souls that were slain because of the Word of God and because of their testimony. These are martyrs who many refer to as tribulation saints, since they died in the tribulation itself.

In verse 10, there is a cry for justice made by the tribulation saints asking the Lord for justice for their deaths. This means that the souls of these believers were on the earth even after the church was removed. Due to their cry for the Lord to avenge their blood, it tells us that identifying as a Christian during the tribulation is dangerous and makes them a target for persecution.

In response, Christ tells them in verse 11 after giving each soul white robes that they should wait a little while longer because more martyrs had to be killed in order to reach a certain number. So this group of martyred saints in heaven is just the first of many groups to be killed for their belief in the gospel of Jesus Christ. The martyrdom of these saints is backed by Daniel 7:24–25 which reads:

> The ten horns are ten kings who will come from this kingdom. After them another king will arise, different from the earlier ones; he will subdue three kings. He will speak against the Most High and oppress his holy people and try to change the set times and the laws. The holy people will be delivered into his hands for a time, times and half a time.

The Sixth Seal

Chapter 6:12–14 details the breaking of the sixth seal, which is where we begin to see the increasing severity of God's judgment on earth. It shows us the first of many other cataclysmic destructions that are to take place on the earth physically. The sixth seal brings with it:

- a massive earthquake
- the sun being made black
- the moon turning blood red
- stars of heaven falling to the earth
- the sky splits
- mountains and islands are moved out of place

Similar to the birth pangs mentioned earlier, the judgments of tribulation come in waves with a climatic series of events at the end of each wave. Besides the earthquake, the other judgments are more supernatural, which will begin to get the attention of both believers and nonbelievers alike.

It's important to note that when Revelation 6:13 mentions stars falling to earth, it's not describing the huge balls of energy in the sky at night. Our closest star is the sun, and it's too huge to be seen "falling" to earth. Therefore, from the perspective of someone standing on earth, a meteor shower would be the closest description to stars falling to earth. And ironically, meteor showers have become more frequent in the past few decades, some making catastrophic impacts in some parts of the earth.

Revelation 6:15–17 gives us a glimpse of how the supernatural judgments will affect everyone on earth, the rich and the poor alike. Verse 15 tells us that "the kings of the earth, the princes, the generals, the rich, the mighty, and everyone else, both slave and free, hid in caves and among the rocks of the mountains."

And it's easy to see why they would want to flee underground from those terrible earthquakes, the blackened sun, and the meteor showers. Scientists have already predicted that if the sun were to stop shining, the earth's temperature would plunge to −100 °F in a matter of days. The atmosphere would undergo violent reactions such as severe tectonic plate movement caused by the dramatic cooling of earth's surface.

Those who sought to hide in underground bunkers are seen to be calling for the rocks and mountains to fall on them so they can hide from the wrath of the Lamb. It would appear that the inhabitants of the earth now recognize that the day of God's wrath has come, and they cannot escape it!

End-of-Chapter Quiz

1. Who is the rider on the white horse that rides out after the first seal is broken?
2. Who are the riders of the red, black, and pale horses?
3. Which horse kills one fourth of mankind on earth?
4. Who were the souls that John saw under the altar of God?
5. What earthly damage does the sixth seal cause?

Answers

1. The rider on the white horse is thought to be the Antichrist because his ambitions are to conquer the world. He represents a military and political power.
2. The red, black, and pale horses are also thought to be the Antichrist who brings war, famine, death, and hell to the world.
3. The pale horse, released by the fourth seal, kills one fourth of mankind.

4. They are the tribulation saints who were martyred for the Word of God.
5. The sixth seal causes a massive earthquake, meteor impact on earth, islands to be displaced, and a drop in temperature because of a darkened sun.

OUR RESPONSIBILITY TO SHARE THE WORD OF GOD

> *"Then he said to them, 'Go into all the world and preach the gospel to all creation.'"*
>
> — MARK 16:15

I'm dedicated to sharing the word of God, not just because I want to help other people find the love and happiness I've experienced in my own life as a result of my faith, but because it's something the Bible clearly shows us that Jesus asks us to do. We are to be the catalyst for a change of heart in others as we share God's message and lead them toward His light.

It is a responsibility for those of us who have experienced God's grace to share His word and encourage more people into fellowship with him. When we follow the word of God and share His message, His Spirit will guide us... and with that knowledge in our hearts, it's virtually impossible not to want to share the good news – particularly in trying times when we know our neighbors are struggling.

Jesus is the only way to eternal life in Heaven... It's no wonder that I want to spread His teachings far and wide and help as many people as I can to access that beautiful promise.

And this is your chance to join me in spreading the word.

By leaving a review of this book on Amazon, you'll show new readers the way to understanding the Book of Revelation and feeling the guiding light of God.

Simply by letting other readers know how this book has helped you and what you've found within it, you'll be playing your part in sharing the word of God, helping more people find His love.

Thank you so much for your support. I'm passionate about bringing His message to as many people as I can; when we work together, we can reach far more people.

Scan the QR code below for a quick review!

7

REVELATION 7—THE 144,000 SEALED OF ISRAEL

REVELATION 7:1–17

144,000 Sealed

After this I saw four angels standing at the four corners of the earth, holding back the four winds of the earth to prevent any wind from blowing on the land or on the sea or on any tree. Then I saw another angel coming up from the east, having the seal of the living God. He called out in a loud voice to the four angels who had been given power to harm the land and the sea: "Do not harm the land or the sea or the trees until we put a seal on the foreheads of the servants of our God." Then I heard the number of those who were sealed: 144,000 from all the tribes of Israel. From the tribe of Judah 12,000 were sealed, from the tribe of Reuben 12,000, from the tribe of Gad 12,000, from the tribe of Asher 12,000, from the tribe of Naphtali 12,000, from the tribe of Manasseh 12,000, from the tribe of Simeon 12,000, from the tribe of Levi 12,000, from the tribe of Issachar 12,000, from the tribe of Zebulun 12,000, from the tribe of Joseph 12,000, from the tribe of Benjamin 12,000.

The Great Multitude in White Robes

After this I looked, and there before me was a great multitude that no one could count, from every nation, tribe, people and language, standing before the throne and before the Lamb. They were wearing white robes and were holding palm branches in their hands. And they cried out in a loud voice: "Salvation belongs to our God, who sits on the throne, and to the Lamb." All the angels were standing around the throne and around the elders and the four living creatures. They fell down on their faces before the throne and worshiped God, saying: "Amen! Praise and glory and wisdom and thanks and honor and power and strength be to our God for ever and ever. Amen!" Then one of the elders asked me, "These in white robes—who are they, and where did they come from?" I answered, "Sir, you know." And he said, "These are they who have come out of the great tribulation; they have washed their robes and made them white in the blood of the Lamb. Therefore, "they are before the throne of God and serve him day and night in his temple; and he who sits on the throne will shelter them with his presence. 'Never again will they hunger; never again will they thirst. The sun will not beat down on them,' nor any scorching heat. For the Lamb at the center of the throne will

> be their shepherd; 'he will lead them to springs of living water.' 'And God will wipe away every tear from their eyes.'"

Revelation 7:1–3 Revealed

If you look carefully at Revelation 7:1–3, it may appear to be a continuation of the events from Chapter 6, although it's an entirely different scenario. The tribulation is rife with various breathtaking events that all seem to be happening simultaneously, making it somewhat complex for readers. Actually, some of these events do happen simultaneously. But we'll take our time in dissecting the scripture so we don't get confused.

Undeniably, the events in Chapter 7 verse 1 are happening at the same time as those in Chapter 6 judging from the context.

John recounts seeing four angels standing at the four corners of the earth holding back the four winds of the earth. The angels are preventing the winds from blowing on the land, the sea, or the trees. This is in contrast to what was said in Chapter 6 about earthquakes, figurative stars falling to earth, and mountains being shaken from their foundations. So it appears that the events of Chapter 7 predate those of Chapter 6. If the angels were to cause the winds on earth to stop blowing, there would be catastrophic consequences from that alone. The earth's weather and water cycle is driven by wind, so we're talking global drought, famine, and starvation.

Proceeding to verse 2, another angel is seen rising from the east and instructing the other four angels not to begin executing their judgments on earth until the servants of Jesus Christ are sealed on their foreheads.

A seal is another word for mark, and the mark of a believer is to be born again and filled with the Holy Spirit. Sealing the bond servants on their foreheads is also a strategic act, and we'll see why later in the tribulation when the Antichrist makes it mandatory for every person on earth to receive a mark on their foreheads to distinguish them as his own.

Revelation 7:4–8 Revealed

So in the midst of the Antichrist rising to power and the Lord stopping the wind to usher in the physical earthly judgments, He will also be nurturing a new generation of believers even after the church has been removed prior to the tribulation. John reveals the identity of these remnant believers in Revelation 7:4–8. They are the 144,000 tribulation saints from each of the 12 tribes of the sons of Israel which consists of the following:

- Judah: 12,000
- Reuben: 12,000
- Gad: 12,000
- Asher: 12,000
- Naphtali: 12,000
- Manasseh: 12,000
- Simeon: 12,000
- Levi: 12,000
- Issachar: 12,000
- Zebulun: 12,000

- Joseph: 12,000
- Benjamin: 12,000

Over the years, there has been much speculation over the true identity of the 144,000, with the entire non-Christian religious organizations being formed off the basis that they are the embodiment of these tribulation saints, such as the Jehovah's Witnesses. But these arguments are futile because the proof is in the pudding or, rather, in the scriptures. The text lets us know that:

- the 144,000 bond servants of Christ come to faith after the start of the tribulation
- people will have a chance to believe in Christ even after the rapture has taken place and the church has been removed
- the 144,000 are taken from among the 12 tribes of Israel, making them all Jewish
- believers who are part of the church body before the start of tribulation cannot be part of the 144,000 according to the Scripture

If you're a true student of the Bible, you may have realized that there were originally 13 tribes of Israel, but the tribe of Dan is missing from the 144,000 tribe list. That's likely because the tribe of Dan has been excluded due to being the first tribe to introduce idolatry into Israel. It is also suggested by some historians and Bible scholars that the Antichrist will come from the tribe of Dan, although this has not been considered by mainstream sources.

In God's great mercy, he personally converts the souls of the 144,000 to become the new pioneers of faith in Jesus during the tribulation. They will be responsible for igniting a new wave of faith on earth after the rapture takes place.

Revelation 7:9–12 Revealed

Revelation 7:9 begins with John witnessing a great multitude of believers standing before the throne and the Lamb. Although this passage is connected to the first half of Chapter 7, it's clear that this multitude is different from the 144,000 because the text expressly says, "After this I looked, and there before me was a great multitude that no one could count, from every nation, tribe, people and language."

- In addition to them being an uncountable crowd, they are in heaven and not on earth like the 144,000, which leads us to believe that they could represent those who have died in Christ.
- They are clothed in white robes and have palm branches in their hands, which clearly points to them being believers.
- They come from every nation, tribe, people, and tongue which disqualifies them from being the 144,000 from the tribes of Israel.

This multinational group of believers also joins in the praises to God on the throne and the Lamb along with the angels, the elders, and the four living creatures, similar to what happened in Chapter 4 and 5. They are singing, praising, glorifying, and blessing the Father and are noticeably joyful to have escaped the hell on earth they left behind. That is expressed in Revelation 7:13–17.

Revelation 7:13–17 Revealed

As if asking a rhetorical question, one of the elders asked John in Revelation 7:13 if he knew where the people clothed in white robes came from, to which John replied that the elder already knew the answer to that question. The elder then replied in confirmation that the multitude he sees are those who came out of great tribulation and have made their robes white in the blood of the Lamb.

We are told that these believers came out of great tribulation, which means the Antichrist was already ruling at this time. For such a grand multitude of bond servants to be in heaven means that a large portion of them were martyred on earth. It only confirms that being a believer during the tribulation is dangerous and that many who come to Christ during the tribulation will be killed for their faith. There is therefore no doubt that both evangelism and martyrdom will be themes throughout the entire book of Revelation.

We can be sure of this because of what is mentioned in verse 15, which says that washing their clothes in the blood of the Lamb, or putting on Christ, is the reason they are before God's throne and worship Him continually in His temple. Revelation 7:16–17 gives us an idea of why the multitude in white robes are so joyful to be martyred and in heaven:

> Never again will they hunger; never again will they thirst. The sun will not beat down on them, nor any scorching heat. For the Lamb at the center of the throne will be their shepherd; he will lead them to springs of living water. And God will wipe away every tear from their eyes.

This describes a much better eternal existence than spending another second being persecuted by the Antichrist and his demonic army. As we've come to the end of the sixth seal being opened, the focus is on the 144,000 chosen vessels who will be spreading the faith of Jesus Christ while in the tribulation. There is more to be revealed about the characteristics of the 144,000 in the later chapters. But before that, let's head over to Chapter 8 for the breaking of the seventh seal.

End-of-Chapter Quiz

1. Who are the 144,000?
2. What would happen on earth if the wind stopped blowing, as we read in verse 1?
3. Which tribe is missing from the 12 tribes listed for the 144,000 and why?
4. Why were the angels told in verse 3 not to harm the land or the sea?
5. What is the mission of the 144,000?

Answers

1. The 144,000 consist of 12,000 male Jews from each of the 12 tribes of Israel.
2. The world would be plunged into famine, drought, and starvation since the water cycle depends on the wind.
3. The tribe of Dan is excluded possibly because it was the first tribe to introduce idolatry to Israel in the Old Testament.

4. The angel instructed them not to harm the land or sea until the 144,000 servants of God were sealed.
5. After the rapture of the church, the 144,000 will be God's firstfruits or remnants on earth during the reign of the Antichrist.

8

REVELATION 8: THE SEVENTH SEAL

REVELATION 8:1–13

The Seventh Seal and the Golden Censer

When he opened the seventh seal, there was silence in heaven for about half an hour. And I saw the seven angels who stand before God, and seven trumpets were given to them. Another angel, who had a golden censer, came and stood at the altar. He was given much incense to offer, with the prayers of all God's people, on the golden altar in front of the throne. The smoke of the incense, together with the prayers of God's people, went up before God from the angel's hand. Then the angel took the censer, filled it with fire from the altar, and hurled it on the earth; and there came peals of thunder, rumblings, flashes of lightning and an earthquake.

The Trumpets

Then the seven angels who had the seven trumpets prepared to sound them. The first angel sounded his trumpet, and there came hail and fire mixed with blood, and it was hurled down on the earth. A third of the earth was burned up, a third of the trees were burned up, and all the green grass was burned up. The second angel sounded his trumpet, and something like a huge mountain, all ablaze, was thrown into the sea. A third of the sea turned into blood, a third of the living creatures in the sea died, and a third of the ships were destroyed. The third angel sounded his trumpet, and a great star, blazing like a torch, fell from the sky on a third of the rivers and on the springs of water—the name of the star is Wormwood. A third of the waters turned bitter, and many people died from the waters that had become bitter. The fourth angel sounded his trumpet, and a third of the sun was struck, a third of the moon, and a third of the stars, so that a third of them turned dark. A third of the day was without light, and also a third of the night. As I watched, I heard an eagle that was flying in midair call out in a loud voice: "Woe! Woe! Woe to the inhabitants of the earth, because of the trumpet blasts about to be sounded by the other three angels!"

Revelation 8:1–4 Revealed

We've covered quite a bit in the Book of Revelation up to this point. The story continues to unfold as the final seven years of Daniel's 70 sevens are made manifest, also known as Jacob's trouble.

We also discussed the signs of the end of the age, such as the birth pangs of earthquakes, wars, famines, and pestilence, which includes the church's removal prior to the tribulation.

Now that six of the seven seals on the land deed scroll have been broken, the judgments of tribulation have been set into motion.

- We've seen the four horsemen of the Apocalypse begin their strategic reign of terror, which represents the Antichrist's rise to power.
- With the power he has been given, he incites wars causing mass destruction, devastation, and starvation.
- Billions out of the world population are set to die because of disease and hyperinflation, leading to starvation.

Chapter 7 then presents us with the 144,000 tribulation saints which we are told are all Jewish men from the 12 tribes of Israel. These men are to reach the world with the gospel of Jesus Christ after the church has been raptured, a world that is governed by the Antichrist and is intolerant of Christians. Because of this, they are martyred, an end many believers in the tribulation will have to face.

However, it's in the sixth seal that we start to witness the supernatural, cataclysmic destruction both in the heavens and on the earth. From mountain-shifting earthquakes to a blackened sun and a blood-red moon, the sneak preview to God's awesome and fearsome power is on open display. And it's going to continue with the seventh seal.

The Seventh Seal

Revelation 8:1 begins with Christ breaking the seventh seal followed by silence in heaven for half an hour. This period of silence only serves to accentuate the magnitude of the judgments that are to be unleashed. We can't forget the number seven means 100% or completion. What is about to be released will strike dread and terror into the hearts of every nonbeliever.

There is a resurgence of the number seven in verse 2 as John sees the seven angels who stand before God holding seven trumpets.

But before that occurs, we are briefly taken back to Revelation 5:8 where there is a connection between the golden bowls of incense that act as the prayers of the saints mentioned again in Revelation 8:3. We find that another angel is seen standing at the altar holding a golden censer with much incense, which he adds to the prayers of the saints on the altar mentioned in Revelation 5:8.

Once the angel has mixed the prayers of the saints with the smoke of the incense, it rises to God's throne. It's assumed that these are prayers for the Lord's protection and defense from what they are experiencing and about to experience as the seven angels are preparing to sound the seven trumpets that will bring the next wave of judgment. The trumpet warnings precede the bowl judgments, which are the third woe judgments, and act as the greatest, most destructive of all the previous judgments.

Revelation 8:5–6 Revealed

But before the trumpet judgments begin, the angel holding the bowl of incense and the prayers of the saints throws it to the earth. This was followed by peals of thunder, flashes of lightning, and an earthquake. Christ Himself warned of frequent earthquakes as a sign of impending judgment on the Mount of Olives, and they are sure to increase in intensity throughout the Book of Revelation.

Once the bowl of prays and incense has been emptied onto the earth, Revelation 8:6 tells us that the seven angels with the seven trumpets prepare themselves to sound. And this is where the physical earth changes make it impossible to deny the hand of God shaking things up.

Revelation 8:7 Revealed

At the sound of the first trumpet in Revelation 8:7, it produced a judgment of hail mixed with fire and blood that was hurled to the earth, prompting one third of the trees and forestation to be burned up. Further evidence later in the Book of Revelation supports the idea that one third of the land on Earth will actually be uninhabitable. The damage will be reserved to a specific area on Earth.

As it was in the beginning, so shall it be in the end. There seems to be a parallel here between the judgments that were loosed by God to bring Israel out of their physical bondage in Egypt and the supernatural judgments in the tribulation in which the church is being delivered from sin in spiritual Egypt. There were also great signs and wonders accompanying the Israelites' transition from Egypt, like in Exodus 9:23: "When Moses stretched out his staff toward the sky, the LORD sent thunder and hail, and lightning flashed down to the ground. So the LORD rained hail on the land of Egypt."

Revelation 8:8–9 Revealed

Moving forward to Revelation 8:8, John describes seeing a great mountain burning with fire be thrown into the sea, turning one third of it into blood. Continuing on into verse 9, we're told that a third of the living creatures in the sea died along with one third of the ships being destroyed. Remember, John is relaying what he is seeing in a vision, so, of course, there are no mountains falling from the sky into the sea in waking life. A sea volcano or a giant falling meteor might be a close-enough description, considering the fact that one third of the animals in the sea perished. But, on the contrary, meteors and volcanos don't turn the sea blood red.

However, this isn't the first time in the Bible we've seen the water turn to blood. This second trumpet judgment again reminds us of the Book of Exodus, where the Lord turned the Nile to blood, and in similar fashion, it killed the fish therein. Similarly, we can be sure that John's account of the sea turning to blood is true and killing one third of the marine life is factual since it happened once before as a form of judgment to Pharaoh.

Except this time, it's not limited to the Nile River but to one third of a body of water. In the same way that the Lord released judgment in Egypt to prove a point, He is also proving a point by incrementally diminishing the habitable areas of the earth, especially in the west. The events of tribulation will eventually lead to the Middle East, where the final battle between Jerusalem and Babylon will take place.

Revelation 8:10–11 Revealed

As we continue on Revelation 8:10–11, we'll soon learn that the signs in the heavens become increasingly fantastic and downright scary. As the third angel blows his trumpet, John describes seeing "a great star, blazing like a torch, fell from the sky on a third of the rivers and on the springs of water." But this star has a name —Wormwood. The name "Wormwood" in Greek means bitter, and this bitterness infects a third of the waters which caused many men to die.

Being that the text refers to Wormwood as a star, we can assume that it's a literal star. But the likelihood of a star even half the size of the sun striking Earth leaves little hope for humanity. Star is also used to refer to angels, whether good or bad. It's possible that Wormwood is a fallen angel entity commissioned by God to do His bidding as part of His judgment, like causing men to die from bitter water.

Revelation 8:12 Revealed

John's gaze is fixed on heaven as the fourth angel sounds the trumpet, which causes a third of the sun, a third of the moon, and a third of the stars to be struck. This would result in a third of these heavenly bodies being darkened and withdrawing their shine. What does this mean?

- John writes that one third of the sun, moon, and stars would be darkened, meaning that they would be shining for one third less time than they normally would.

- This means that the earth would be receiving one third less energy from those heavenly bodies.
- Naturally, since the moon reflects the light of the sun, if the sun shines for one third less of the day, the moon will shine one third less at night.
- Less energy from the sun would result in a drop in temperature, leading to massive crop failure, frozen water sources, and dying livestock.

Revelation 8:13 Revealed

After such a massive blow to the earth and the universe in Revelation 8:12, the trumpet judgments are temporarily suspended to allow for a warning to be given to earth in Revelation 8:13.

- John sees an angel flying in midheaven proclaiming a warning for more impending judgment.
- Since there were no Hebrew words to differentiate the three "heavens," they were described as first heaven being where the birds flew, the second or midheaven being where the stars and planets dwelled, and the third heaven being God's dwelling place.

John sees an eagle in midheaven, but eagles don't fly among the planets. So it was more than likely an angel circling back and forth while proclaiming the warning: "Woe! Woe! Woe to the inhabitants of the earth, because of the trumpet blasts about to be sounded by the other three angels" (Revelation 8:13).

"Woe" describes a horrible period. The heavenly being proclaims woe three times, essentially stating that the fifth, sixth, and seventh trumpets are the three woes, which will be exceedingly terrible for those on earth. The third woe judgment will declare the pouring out of the bowl judgments, which means you can expect some of God's mightiest and most dreadful acts to be performed.

Now that we've covered the events surrounding the seventh seal and the first four trumpet blast judgments, we're starting to see the similarities between the Israelites' exodus from Egypt, the mighty acts of God that accompanied their move, and the hatred of Pharaoh alongside the hatred of Christians during the tribulation, the church's exodus to heaven, the hardness of the Antichrist's heart, and the epic judgments that accompany these events.

We'll press forward with the remainder of the trumpet blasts and the other three woes. Prepare for more mind-blowing revelations!

End-of-Chapter Quiz

1. What does the angel in verse 3 offer up to God as incense in the golden censer before the altar?
2. What happened after the angel holding the golden censer threw the incense and the prayers to the earth?
3. What happened when the first angel sounded his trumpet?
4. How is the judgment of the second trumpet similar to the judgments of Egypt in the Book of Exodus?
5. Who or what is Wormwood?

Answers

1. The prayers of the saints are offered up as incense before God.
2. There are peals of thunder, lightning, and earthquakes. Then the seven angels get ready to sound their trumpet.
3. Hail and fire mixed with blood was thrown to the earth, burning up one third of the trees and grass on earth.
4. In both events, the sea turned to blood, and the animals in the water died.
5. Wormwood is mentioned as a star, or an angel, that fell from heaven and turned the rivers and springs of water bitter, causing men to die.

9

REVELATION 9—THE TRUMPETS

REVELATION 9:1–21

The fifth angel sounded his trumpet, and I saw a star that had fallen from the sky to the earth. The star was given the key to the shaft of the Abyss. When he opened the Abyss, smoke rose from it like the smoke from a gigantic furnace. The sun and sky were darkened by the smoke from the Abyss. And out of the smoke locusts came down on the earth and were given power like that of scorpions of the earth. They were told not to harm the grass of the earth or any plant or tree, but only those people who did not have the seal of God on their foreheads. They were not allowed to kill them but only to torture them for five months. And the agony they suffered was like that of the sting of a scorpion when it strikes. During those days people will seek death but will not find it; they will long to die, but death will elude them. The locusts looked like horses prepared for battle. On their heads they wore something like crowns of gold, and their faces resembled human faces. Their hair was like women's hair, and their teeth were like lions' teeth. They had breastplates like breastplates of iron, and the sound of their wings was like the thundering of many horses and chariots rushing into battle. They had tails with stingers, like scorpions, and in their tails they had power to torment people for five months. They had as king over them the angel of the Abyss, whose name in Hebrew is Abaddon and in Greek is Apollyon (that is, Destroyer). The first woe is past; two other woes are yet to come. The sixth angel sounded his trumpet, and I heard a voice coming from the four horns of the golden altar that is before God. It said to the sixth angel who had the trumpet, "Release the four angels who are bound at the great river Euphrates." And the four angels who had been kept ready for this very hour and day and month and year were released to kill a third of mankind. The number of the mounted troops was twice ten thousand times ten thousand. I heard their number. The horses and riders I saw in my vision looked like this: Their breastplates were fiery red, dark blue, and yellow as sulfur. The heads of the horses resembled the heads of lions, and out of their mouths came fire, smoke and sulfur. A third of mankind was killed by the three plagues of fire, smoke and sulfur that came out of their mouths. The power of the horses was in their mouths and in their tails; for their tails were like snakes, having heads with which they inflict injury. The rest of mankind who were not killed by these plagues still did not repent of the work of their hands; they did not

> stop worshiping demons, and idols of gold, silver, bronze, stone and wood—idols that cannot see or hear or walk. Nor did they repent of their murders, their magic arts, their sexual immorality or their thefts.

Revelation 9:1–6 Revealed

The text starts in Revelation 9:1 with John recounting what he envisioned after the fifth angel sounded his trumpet. He clearly sees a star which fell from heaven to earth and was then given the key to the bottomless pit. Sounds a bit frightening, doesn't it? The first thing we recognize is that unlike Chapter 8 where John speaks of a star called Wormwood crashing to earth, it's unmistakable that the star mentioned in this text is an angel since we read, "The key of the bottomless pit was given to him" (*New American Standard Bible*, 1995, Revelation 9:1). The use of "him" makes it clear that this star is a person, not an object like a burning mountain of meteor.

We're aware that the word "star" is often used to describe an angel. But this angel falls from heaven, making him a fallen angel.

- Further along in verse 11, we'll see that this fallen angel is given the name Abaddon or Apollyon.
- The word Apollyon in Greek means destroyer, which is one of the characteristics of Satan, who, coincidentally, was once an angel in heaven named Lucifer until he was banished by the Father for leading a revolt in heaven. This is also a confirmation that this is not a benevolent being.

The fallen angel opens the bottomless pit with the key he was given, which releases such a great smoke that it even darkens the sun and the atmosphere. Revelation 9:3 shows us that out of the smoke of the bottomless pit, or the abyss, came grotesque locusts upon the earth. For a better understanding of the types of creatures being released, the Greek word for bottomless used in this text is *abussos*, which literally means abyss.

This bottomless pit, also known as Sheol or Hades, is mentioned in other parts of the Bible, such as in 2 Peter 2:4–5:

> For if God did not spare angels when they sinned, but sent them to hell, putting them in chains of darkness to be held for judgment; if he did not spare the ancient world when he brought the flood on its ungodly people, but protected Noah, a preacher of righteousness, and seven others.

If you were wondering where locusts with the deadly and venomous power of a scorpion were being released from, here's your answer. This was some sort of prison for the souls of deceased unbelievers as well as for the spirits of rebellious fallen angels. However, not all demons or fallen angels are stuck in Sheol; otherwise, there would be no demon possessions. But some of the worst fallen angels were held captive, and now this chief demon named Apollyon was allowed to release them.

The malevolent locust beings have been caged for thousands of years and are eager to wreak havoc on mankind, for it is their appointed time to do so. But these aren't your average, crop-eating locusts. As a matter of fact, they operate opposite to earthly locusts. Proof of this is found in Revelation 9:4 where the locusts are instructed not to harm the grass or any vegetation on the earth, but they are permitted to harm the men who aren't marked with the seal of God.

They are further instructed in verse 5 not to kill the men but only torture them for five months, and their torment is like that of a scorpion when it stings a man. Notice that only the men without God's seal on their foreheads (bringing us back to the 144,000) will be tortured by the locusts.

By allowing this, God is making a clear distinction between the godly and the ungodly, the latter of whom will be the only group receiving His judgment. And the penalty is quite painful as we know that scorpions are known for their toxic stings, although they're not fatal. We get a clearer understanding of how severe this judgment is in Revelation 9:6 where we're told that men will seek death to relieve the torturous pain from the locusts but won't be able to die. Death will literally be avoiding them.

When John says "they will long to die" in verse 6, the word "long" in Greek means to crave or desire. The real question is why aren't these men able to kill themselves to end their painful misery? A possible reason is that the locust torture is so severe that they are rendered immobile by the pain and don't even have the strength to harm themselves. Remember, even though the five-month locust torture is compared to the sting of a scorpion, the attack is coming from demonic creatures that have been imprisoned for thousands of years with a vendetta against mankind. So the pain will hit differently.

Revelation 9:7–11 Revealed

Let's not forget that John is doing his best to relay what is being depicted in the vision he's beholding, so we can't expect these creatures to be true scorpions or locusts. Perhaps the sting of a scorpion was used in his description because scorpions were even used by Jesus to describe demonic entities, such as in Luke 10:19: "I have given you authority to trample on snakes and scorpions and to overcome all the power of the enemy; nothing will harm you."

Even John's physical description of these creatures is nothing like that of a scorpion nor a locust. He says in Revelation 9:7 that the locusts looked like horses prepared for battle; they had the heads of men, equipped with hair like a woman and teeth like a lion. There also appeared to be golden crowns on their heads, signifying a level of authority in the demonic kingdom.

He also mentions in verses 9–10 that they have on breastplates of iron, their wings produce the powerful sound of horses rushing into battle, and their tails are like unto scorpion's tails. And actually, this is where they sting and hurt men for five months. Now we know why John compared these creatures to scorpions—their tails are the only thing in their description that looks remotely "scorpion." But the iron breastplate, long hair, lion-like teeth, and powerful wings sound like something out of a Stephen King movie.

The icing on the cake that lets us know the nature of these creatures and the identity of the angel with the key who released them is found in Revelation 9:11 which states that there was a king over them, who is the angel of the abyss. That would confirm that the "star" which fell from heaven with the key to the bottomless pit is indeed the angel spoken of in this verse. It goes on to call this "angel of the abyss" by his Hebrew name, *Abaddon*, or in Greek, *Apollyon*. As we've covered previously, the definition of both of those names means destroyer. It's then safe to say that all hell has literally broken loose on earth, specifically on those who don't bear God's seal upon them, for at least five months.

Revelation 9:12 Revealed

Then Revelation 9:12 informs us that after the five months, the first woe is past. But there are yet two woes impending to be released. Biblically, five is the number for grace. So despite the horrendous torture those without God's seal had to endure, His mercy was still shown by not allowing death to prevail. It's as if they were served a taste of hell at the hands of demons, but their souls were spared from eternal damnation.

Revelation 9:13–19 Revealed

As promised, the second woe would be equal to, if not more severe than, the first woe we covered in Chapter 9 verses 1–6. Beginning in Revelation 9:13, the sixth angel sounded his trumpet, marking the start of the second woe. And in keeping with the trend of releasing the fallen angels, we read that one of the four horns of God's golden altar instructs the angel with the trumpet to release the four angels bound at the great river Euphrates. Here, we see for the second time that even the wicked fallen angels are being used to bring about God's purpose.

The next verse says that these angels were bound for a season and were set to be released for a specific date and time and for a specific function. That function is to kill a third of mankind. Realize that just as when the seventh seal was released previously in Revelation 8 and one third of the trees were burned up, one third of the sea became blood, one third of the ships were destroyed, and one third of the water became bitter as wormwood; one third of mankind is to be killed by these fallen angels.

It's clear that the grace period is over and the death of mankind is now an option. The death of so many people is determined to come by way of the armies of 200 million horsemen. John then confirms that he heard the number of the horsemen. But what horsemen are these? Some suggest it to be an antagonistic human army that will accomplish the killings. But, for argument's sake, let's say the Chinese army could be responsible. Surely, they can recruit 200 million soldiers, but where can they find that many horses? After all, John said they were horsemen.

In addition, the description John gives us of the riders in verse 17 of having breastplates the color of fire, hyacinth, and brimstone and the heads of lions doesn't sound like the average human soldier. In fact, they sound like creatures out of the movie *Fantastic Beasts*. Out of the riders' mouths also issues fire, smoke, and brimstone.

The description sounds similar to the imagery of the locusts in Revelation 9:7 which describes the locusts as "horses prepared for battle." We can then suggest that the 200 million horsemen John saw were more demonic creatures that were summoned by the four fallen angels.

As promised, we learn in Revelation 9:18–19 that a third of mankind was killed by the smoke, fire, and brimstone, which represented the three plagues that came from the mouths of the horsemen. We are also informed that the power of the horses is in their mouths and in their serpent-like tails. And since there is nothing in the text that suggests these descriptions should be taken symbolically, the horsemen should be taken for what they are—demonic beings sent to kill humanity.

Revelation 9:20–21 Revealed

In several places in the Bible, the Lord uses suffering to bring people to a place of repentance and faith. Many times, the judgment itself is an act of God's mercy, especially if He has tried gentler approaches that were ignored. The same can be said for the first two woes. We discussed what happened when the fifth angel sounded its trumpet and saw that demonic creatures were released by Wormwood and tortured men for five months without death. That was God's mercy on display.

But we see in Revelation 9:20–21 that even after the sixth angel sounded the trumpet and a worse judgment befell the earth, this time killing a third of mankind, those who were not killed by the plagues (smoke, fire, and brimstone) still did not repent of their idolatry, their murders, or any other immoralities they committed. For them to not have repented means that the option was available for repentance, which is the result of the 144,000 being present. The woe judgments, which are undoubtedly a supernatural occurrence, were meant to draw in unbelievers by His grace. But as Scripture tells us, unless a person answers the knock of God on the door of their hearts, there is no other way they will turn to Him.

The mere fact that, despite the numerous unconventional ways God tries to get the attention of unbelievers, they refuse to put their faith in Him shines light on the text in Ephesians 2:8–9: "For it is by grace you have been saved, through faith—and this is not from yourselves, it is the gift of God—not by works, so that no one can boast."

God doesn't want to scare us into having faith in Him because faith isn't based on fear.

With Chapter 9 now complete, we've come to the end of the first half of the tribulation. That means three and a half years of the seven-year tribulation is through, and there are three and a half more years left. So far, the seal and trumpet judgments are complete with only one final trumpet judgment left, which make up the seven bowl judgments. Prepare yourselves because things are about to get worse before they get better.

End-of-Chapter Quiz

1. What is the name of the star that fell from heaven in verse 1, and what does it mean?
2. What key does the angel have in his possession?
3. What is released from the abyss when it is opened?
4. What is the purpose of the abyss in the Bible?
5. What happens when the four fallen angels are released from the river Euphrates?

Answers

1. The name of the star, or angel, is Abaddon in Hebrew or Apollyon in Greek and means destroyer.
2. The angel is given the key to the bottomless pit or the abyss.
3. Demonic creatures that look like locust hybrids are released from the abyss.
4. The abyss, the bottomless pit, is used as holding prison for demons and fallen angels.
5. The four fallen angels kill one third of mankind.

10

REVELATION 10—THE ANGEL AND THE BOOK

REVELATION 10:1–11

The Angel and the Little Scroll

Then I saw another mighty angel coming down from heaven. He was robed in a cloud, with a rainbow above his head; his face was like the sun, and his legs were like fiery pillars. He was holding a little scroll, which lay open in his hand. He planted his right foot on the sea and his left foot on the land, and he gave a loud shout like the roar of a lion. When he shouted, the voices of the seven thunders spoke. And when the seven thunders spoke, I was about to write; but I heard a voice from heaven say, "Seal up what the seven thunders have said and do not write it down." Then the angel I had seen standing on the sea and on the land raised his right hand to heaven. And he swore by him who lives for ever and ever, who created the heavens and all that is in

> them, the earth and all that is in it, and the sea and all that is in it, and said, "There will be no more delay! But in the days when the seventh angel is about to sound his trumpet, the mystery of God will be accomplished, just as he announced to his servants the prophets." Then the voice that I had heard from heaven spoke to me once more: "Go, take the scroll that lies open in the hand of the angel who is standing on the sea and on the land." So I went to the angel and asked him to give me the little scroll. He said to me, "Take it and eat it. It will turn your stomach sour, but 'in your mouth it will be as sweet as honey.'" I took the little scroll from the angel's hand and ate it. It tasted as sweet as honey in my mouth, but when I had eaten it, my stomach turned sour. Then I was told, "You must prophesy again about many peoples, nations, languages and kings."

Revelation 10:1–7 Revealed

Now that we're midway through the tribulation, we can expect to see more mighty acts from God starting in Revelation 10:1 with "another" angel descending from heaven. Unlike the angels in Chapter 9 who also came to earth from heaven, this angel was not of a fallen nature. Nevertheless, his appearance is intimidating, and he is described as strong with a face like the sun, feet like pillars of fire, and a glorious rainbow on his head. We can discern that this angel was one of great authority in heaven, as he is said to also be "clothed with a cloud."

But besides his resplendent appearance, the most distinct feature of this angel is the little book he carries in his hand or, rather, a book smaller than the size of a scroll. In contrast to the small book in his hand, the angel is quite large in appearance, as we read in Revelation 10:2 that when he arrives on earth, he places one foot on the sea and the other on land. Then we read in verse 3 that as the angel cried out in a loud voice similar to that of a lion's roar, heaven responded with seven voices of thunder.

After the seven thunders spoke, another voice from heaven instructs John to "seal up what the seven thunders have said and do not write it down."

This entire scene, including John being told to seal up what the seven peals of thunder spoke, are reminiscent of Daniel 12:1, which reads:

> At that time Michael, the great prince who protects your people, will arise. There will be a time of distress such as has not happened from the beginning of nations until then. But at that time your people—everyone whose name is found written in the book—will be delivered.

When Daniel started out with "now at that time," it is actually referring to the time of the tribulation, specifically during the rise of the Antichrist. In Daniel 12:4, the prophet is told to conceal the words and seal up the book until the time of the end, similar to what John was told to do in Daniel 10:4.

We also find in Daniel 12:5–9 that he asks the men who were on the opposite banks of a river how long it would be before the words concealed in the book would take place. In response, another man dressed in white linen who was above the waters of the river raised both his hands toward heaven and swore that "it will be for a time, times and half a time" or three and a half years. The angel says further that all these events will take place when the age of the Gentiles is finished or "when the power of the holy people has been finally broken" (Daniel 12:7).

This is almost identical to what the massive angel said in Revelation 10:5–6. Verse 5 says that the angel standing on the sea lifted his right hand to heaven and swore by Him who lives forever that there will be no more delay. It is then made clear that the scroll that Daniel wrote was held by the angel he spoke to until the second half of tribulation, when its contents would be made known to John. And even after they have been made known to John, there are still some things that John must keep concealed concerning the very end of tribulation.

These events won't be fulfilled until the seventh angel sounds his trumpet and the bowl judgments begin to take place. The delay of the words written sealed by Daniel was meant to be revealed to John, who would reveal them to the servants of Jesus Christ for the last days.

Revelation 10:8–11 Revealed

Moving on to Revelation 10:8, we're still on the topic of the little book, or the scroll, that was given to John. A voice from heaven instructs John to take the book out of the hand of the gigantic angel standing on the sea and the land. The scrolls in those days usually came in a papyrus role and were not edible. Nevertheless, the angel instructs John to eat the book, warning him that it will be sweet in his mouth but bitter in his stomach.

While we're not told that this is the definition, it's a very poetic way of describing the bittersweet nature of the prophecy given about God's end-time judgment. It can be sweet for believers because we who are not of this world look forward to leaving its ways and systems behind in anticipation of the age to come. The promises of eternal life, ruling with Christ, and the end of pain, tears, and suffering are all the sweet things believers in Jesus can hope for.

But then the bitter reality settles in that we won't be able to taste this newness without first doing away with the old. Therefore, judgment must be had on the old-world order, which includes the souls of billions of unbelievers facing the penalty for their sin and rebellion against God—both on earth and in eternity. And the discomfort and distress will also be felt by believers in Christ but in a different way. Whereas the world will be facing God's wrath for their immorality, God's people will be facing persecution for their faith in Him.

End-of-Chapter Quiz

1. What is similar about the angel in Daniel 10 and Revelation 10?
2. Why was John instructed to eat the scroll held by the angel?
3. Why was the scroll sweet in John's mouth but bitter in his stomach?
4. What is the name of the angel that arises to defend God's people in Daniel 12:1?

Answers

1. The words the angel told Daniel to seal up in a scroll is what the little book the angel in Revelation is revealing to John. They both confirm that "there will be no more delay."
2. John must still prophesy to other nations and people around the world.
3. The scroll represents prophecies that are yet to happen. They are sweet for the lives of the believer but a bitter reality for those who reject God and choose to live in sin.
4. Archangel Michael is the angel who arises to defend the people of God.

11

REVELATION 11—THE TWO WITNESSES AND THE SEVENTH TRUMPET

REVELATION 11:1–19

The Two Witnesses

I was given a reed like a measuring rod and was told, "Go and measure the temple of God and the altar, with its worshipers. But exclude the outer court; do not measure it, because it has been given to the Gentiles. They will trample on the holy city for 42 months. And I will appoint my two witnesses, and they will prophesy for 1,260 days, clothed in sackcloth." They are "the two olive trees" and the two lampstands, and "they stand before the Lord of the earth." If anyone tries to harm them, fire comes from their mouths and devours their enemies. This is how anyone who wants to harm them must die. They have power to shut up the heavens so that it will not rain during the time they are prophesying; and they have power to turn the waters into blood and to strike the earth with every kind of plague as often as they want. Now when they have finished their testimony, the beast that comes up from the Abyss will attack them, and overpower and kill them. Their bodies will lie in the public square of the great city—which is figuratively called Sodom and Egypt—where also their Lord was crucified. For three and a half days some from every people, tribe, language and nation will gaze on their bodies and refuse them burial. The inhabitants of the earth will gloat over them and will celebrate by sending each other gifts, because these two prophets had tormented those who live on the earth. But after the three and a half days the breath of life from God entered them, and they stood on their feet, and terror struck those who saw them. Then they heard a loud voice from heaven saying to them, "Come up here." And they went up to heaven in a cloud, while their enemies looked on. At that very hour there was a severe earthquake and a tenth of the city collapsed. Seven thousand people were killed in the earthquake, and the survivors were terrified and gave glory to the God of heaven. The second woe has passed; the third woe is coming soon.

The Seventh Trumpet

The seventh angel sounded his trumpet, and there were loud voices in heaven, which said: "The kingdom of the world has become the kingdom of our Lord and of his Messiah, and he will reign for ever and ever." And the twenty-four elders, who were seated on their thrones before God, fell on their faces and worshiped God, saying: "We give thanks to you, Lord God Almighty, the One who is and who was, because

> you have taken your great power and have begun to reign. The nations were angry, and your wrath has come. The time has come for judging the dead, and for rewarding your servants the prophets and your people who revere your name, both great and small— and for destroying those who destroy the earth." Then God's temple in heaven was opened, and within his temple was seen the ark of his covenant. And there came flashes of lightning, rumblings, peals of thunder, an earthquake and a severe hailstorm.

Revelation 11:1–2 Revealed

After John consumes the Book in Revelation 10:10, he is told by the angel that he is to prophesy to many people, nations, tongues, and kings, signifying that the words he ingested from the scroll are for a time to come. Even though the prophecies of Revelation will be centered around Israel, the scope of God's hand over the earth will impact nations, tongues, and kings the world over.

In the next scene, John is told to measure a Jewish temple and be mindful of who worships there. However, there is no mention of specific measurements taken, so this is not the focal point. The highlight here is that there is again a temple in Israel after the last temple was destroyed by the Romans in 70. Although Orthodox Jews have sought to rebuild their temple, those plans have remained dormant for over 2,000 years.

But John's vision tells us prophetically that there will be a time when the temple is rebuilt, giving worshipers a place to worship before God's altar. Its design is made up of an altar in the outside courtyard near the building housing the holy place of the holy of holies. The courtyard housing the holy of holies is surrounded by a wall partitioning the Jews from the Gentiles. This needs to be mentioned because John is told to only measure the courtyard where the worshipers gather around the altar but not the Gentile court.

So in this verse of the Scripture, we learn that in the midst of war and supernatural calamities, Israel is being spared from the impactful judgments happening around the rest of the world. God is doing this not only because Israel is the apple of His eye but because He hopes that the favor they are being shown will prompt them to return.

Verse 2 goes on to inform us that the reason John was told to exclude the outside court that is given to the other nations is because it will be trampled by the Gentiles for 42 months, which is exactly three and a half years. That tells us that this verse of the Scripture is pointing directly to the second half of the tribulation. So everything seems to be right on schedule.

Revelation 11:3–6 Revealed

Without warning, John takes us into another scene introducing two prophets called the two witnesses in verse 3. This topic seems completely left field to present, but it's all related. We're told that the two witnesses will prophesy for 1,260 days, which is calculated to be 42 months or three and a half years. Their ministry consists of them wearing sackcloth and ashes, which is the attire worn by prophets who are in mourning for Israel.

The concept of the two witnesses is taken from the law of the Old Testament and is based on having two or three witnesses before condemnation or settlement of a matter. It says in Deuteronomy 19:15, "One witness is not enough to convict anyone accused of any crime or offense they may have committed. A matter must be established by the testimony of two or three witnesses."

So in the same way that two or three witnesses needed to be present to confirm the offense of someone before they are condemned, the two witnesses' purpose and ministry is to highlight the offense of sin in the world prior to condemnation and judgment. But besides the expectation of judgment, what is the purpose of witnessing?

- One of the biblical purposes of witnessing is to prophesy a message of truth to bring conviction to a person so they can repent and be saved.
- The other purpose is to testify against someone's sin in order to bring conviction and condemnation.

Apply these purposes to the ministry of the two witnesses, and you'll understand why they were sent to prophesy a message of condemnation of the world's sin in hopes of bringing conviction to the hearts of the hearers and ultimately repentance. Playing such an integral part in the Book of Revelation, of course, there are many speculations and theories about the identity of these two powerhouses. Some believe them to be the two Old Testament prophets, Elijah and Enoch, since the Bible records that neither of these men died naturally and were taken to heaven alive.

Verse 4 attributes them to being the two olive trees and two lampstands that stand before the Lord. This description is a direct reference to Zechariah 4:1–3 which reads:

> Then the angel who talked with me returned and woke me up, like someone awakened from sleep. He asked me, "What do you see?" I answered, "I see a solid gold lampstand with a bowl at the top and seven lamps on it, with seven channels to the lamps. Also there are two olive trees by it, one on the right of the bowl and the other on its left."

Then, further down in Zechariah 4:11–14, when the prophet Zechariah asks the Lord who the two olive trees are on either side of the lampstand, the Lord responds that they are the two anointed ones who stand before the Lord of the earth, which is the exact description given of the two witnesses in Revelation 11:4. Zechariah 4:11–14 reads:

> Then I asked the angel, "What are these two olive trees on the right and the left of the lampstand?" Again I asked him, "What are these two olive branches beside the two gold pipes that pour out golden oil?" He replied, "Do you not know what these are?" "No, my lord," I said. So he said, "These are the two who are anointed to serve the Lord of all the earth."

These two carry a lot of weight and are heavily anointed. By saying that they are standing before the Lord of the whole earth means that their impact will be global, even though their ministry will be centered around the temple in the Holy City.

But having such an impact will garner a great deal of attention and opposition, especially since they've been sent to prophesy judgment on a sinful world. So in Revelation 11:5, with the authority they've been given by God, they're given a superpower which allows fire to proceed from their mouths to devour their enemies or anyone who tries to harm them.

The awesomeness doesn't stop there, though. The next verse lets us know that they also have power to stop rain from falling during the time of their prophesying, can turn water blood red, and can strike the earth with plagues as many times as they desire. In this way, their ministry affects everyone on the earth and is also why they have enemies.

For three and a half years until the middle of the tribulation, they are allowed to inflict these judgments on mankind while being protected by God. It's as though God, in His great love and mercy, sends two mouthpieces to basically narrate the natural disasters manifesting across the world while testifying of God's truth, so that everyone knows it is being orchestrated by God Himself.

Revelation 11:7–10 Revealed

The enemy becomes so enraged with the two witnesses that in Revelation 11:7, we read that the beast that comes out of the abyss overcomes and kills them after they're finished prophesying.

- Remember we read about the abyss, or the bottomless pit, back in Chapter 9? The fallen angel named Apollyon was given the key to open the abyss, out of which came horrible, demonic locusts.

- Now we learn that the beast also comes from the abyss and makes war with the two witnesses, overcoming and killing them. We'll learn more about the beast in the coming chapters, but we know for sure that he comes from the demonic kingdom.

The next verse tells us that the bodies of the two witnesses are laid in the street of the city where the Lord was crucified. Although the text calls this city Sodom and Egypt, we know that Jesus was crucified in Jerusalem. However, during the tribulation, the spiritual state of Jerusalem is not holy and is filled with idolatry, likening it to Egypt of the city of Sodom.

Their dead bodies are kept in the street for three and a half days intentionally while people from all nations and tongues gaze upon them. Instead of respecting their corpses with a burial, the people on earth rejoice and turn their deaths into a celebration.

They send gifts to each other as if to show their merriment over the deaths of these two prophets. In case you were wondering why people would be so pleased with their deaths, remember that the two witnesses had power to strike the earth with plagues, drought, and other natural disasters as often as they wished in self-defense. These things obviously affected the inhabitants of earth, who would now blame them for everything bad happening in the world.

Revelation 11:11–13 Revealed

If the superpowers they displayed weren't enough to convince earth's inhabitants that they came from God, the two witnesses strike dread into the hearts of their enemies when God breathes life into their bodies after the three and a half days are over in Revelation 11:11. Not only are the people of earth terrified after having witnessed a resurrection, but they're more afraid that the prophets will resume their ministry and cause more plagues and disasters.

The following chapter says that a loud voice was heard from heaven telling them to "come up here." Then they were taken up by a cloud into heaven in the presence of their enemies. God allowed the death and resurrection of these men in the sight of the whole world to show that they were approved by Him. And now those who celebrated their deaths were in big trouble.

Revelation 11:13 then informs us that in the same hour the two witnesses ascended to heaven, a great earthquake broke forth, killing 7,000 people. Perhaps this earthshaking judgment, added to the supernatural events they witnessed earlier, led the remaining people who were not killed by the earthquake to glorify the God of heaven.

We'll now proceed to the next verse in Revelation 11:14.

Revelation 11:14 Revealed

The ending of the ministry of the two witnesses marked the end of the second woe, as we are told in Revelation 11:14: "The second woe has passed; the third woe is coming soon."

Let's take a brief recap on the first two woes that have been fulfilled:

- The first woe was at the start of Chapter 9 with the demonic locust or scorpion creatures from the abyss.

- The second woe came at the middle of Chapter 9 when the four fallen angels at the Euphrates River were loosed, causing a 200,000-soldier demonic army to take out a third of mankind.

Coming up is the third woe, which will usher in the seven bowls of judgment. The two witnesses have completed their ministry, having died and resurrected in the process. However, before the seven bowl judgments are released, there is a declaration being made in Revelation 11:15.

Revelation 11:15–19 Revealed

Revelation 11:15 begins when the seventh angel sounds his trumpet, which lets us know that the third woe has been signaled to begin and the seven judgment bowls will be poured out. We're now stepping into the latter part of tribulation, and it is announced in heaven that the kingdom of the world has become the kingdom of the Lord Jesus Christ, and His will be an everlasting kingdom.

- This is said beforehand because the seven bowl judgments precede Christ's Second Coming and the establishment of His kingdom on earth.
- The 24 elders even begin to worship God for His faithfulness and the decision to use His great power to reign over the earth.

We're told in verse 19 that the nations became angry because the wrath of God is coming upon them, which refers to the bowl judgments. After that, the dead will be judged, and rewards will be given to the believers.

The chapter ends with verse 19 informing of the temple of God being opened in heaven with the ark of the covenant in that temple, followed by a barrage of natural powers in heaven and on earth.

We're now moving forward into the culmination of the events of the tribulation, which we will shortly find out in Revelation 12—the most difficult and diabolical time for the world.

End-of-Chapter Quiz

1. When do the two witnesses arrive on earth?
2. What are the two witnesses on earth to do?
3. What are some of the special qualities of the two witnesses?
4. Who are the two witnesses?
5. Who kills the two witnesses?

Answers

1. The two witnesses show up at mid-tribulation.
2. The two witnesses are sent to prophesy for 1,260 days, or three and a half years, to convict the world of sin and unrighteousness so people can repent.
3. The two witnesses are able to cause rain to stop falling during their prophesying, turn the water into blood, strike the earth with plagues, and hurl fire from their mouths to defend against their enemies.

4. Their identities are not confirmed in the Scripture, but they are believed to be either Elijah and Enoch or Elijah and Moses.
5. The beast from the abyss, or the bottomless pit, attacks, overpowers, and kills the two witnesses, but they are resurrected after three days.

12

REVELATION 12—THE WOMAN CLOTHED WITH THE SUN, THE CHILD, AND THE DRAGON

REVELATION 12:1–17

The Woman and the Dragon

A great sign appeared in heaven: a woman clothed with the sun, with the moon under her feet and a crown of twelve stars on her head. She was pregnant and cried out in pain as she was about to give birth. Then another sign appeared in heaven: an enormous red dragon with seven heads and ten horns and seven crowns on its heads. Its tail swept a third of the stars out of the sky and flung them to the earth. The dragon stood in front of the woman who was about to give birth, so that it might devour her child the moment he was born. She gave birth to a son, a male child, who "will rule all the nations with an iron scepter." And her child was snatched up to God and to his throne. The woman fled into the wilderness to a place prepared for her by God, where she might be taken care of for 1,260 days. Then war broke out in heaven. Michael and his angels fought against the dragon, and the dragon and his angels fought back. But he was not strong enough, and they lost their place in heaven. The great dragon was hurled down—that ancient serpent called the devil, or Satan, who leads the whole world astray. He was hurled to the earth, and his angels with him. Then I heard a loud voice in heaven say: "Now have come the salvation and the power and the kingdom of our God, and the authority of his Messiah. For the accuser of our brothers and sisters, who accuses them before our God day and night, has been hurled down. They triumphed over him by the blood of the Lamb and by the word of their testimony; they did not love their lives so much as to shrink from death. Therefore rejoice, you heavens and you who dwell in them! But woe to the earth and the sea, because the devil has gone down to you! He is filled with fury, because he knows that his time is short." When the dragon saw that he had been hurled to the earth, he pursued the woman who had given birth to the male child. The woman was given the two wings of a great eagle, so that she might fly to the place prepared for her in the wilderness, where she would be taken care of for a time, times and half a time, out of the serpent's reach. Then from his mouth the serpent spewed water like a river, to overtake the woman and sweep her away with the torrent. But the earth helped the woman by opening its mouth and swallowing the river that the dragon had spewed out of his mouth. Then the dragon was enraged at the woman and went off to wage war against the rest of her offspring—

> those who keep God's commands and hold fast their testimony about Jesus.

Revelation 12:1–5 Revealed

Symbolism has been used all throughout the Bible. But as you might've discovered, it's used much more in the Book of Revelation. With that, we find one of the most popular signs in Revelation 12:1. But what is a sign and how do we decipher its meaning?

A sign is defined as a symbol that represents something in real life. Much like a road sign that communicates to drivers what to anticipate before turning a corner or crossing an intersection, a sign in the Bible gives us a coded idea of something that needs to be interpreted into its true form.

So now that we have a better understanding of biblical signs, let's begin with the sign in Revelation 12:1 which speaks of a woman clothed with the sun, the moon under her feet, and a crown of 12 stars on her head. The second sign is of a child she is pregnant with and is about to give birth to.

With our understanding of signs, we know that neither the woman nor the child is literal. Therefore, they must mean something else. We are given an idea of who the child is in verse 5 which tells us that the woman gave birth to a male child who is to rule all nations with a rod of iron. The man-child is later taken up to heaven and God's throne.

Since we use scripture to reference scripture, we'll look for the connecting text where someone is ruling with a rod of iron, which is found in Psalm 2:7–9:

> I will proclaim the LORD's decree: He said to me, "You are my son; today I have become your father. Ask me, and I will make the nations your inheritance, the ends of the earth your possession. You will break them with a rod of iron; you will dash them to pieces like pottery."

This psalm written by David is actually prophetic and speaks to the return of Jesus Christ to earth to rule with a rod of iron after the tribulation. We can surmise that the child being spoken of is Jesus Christ. But there is further evidence supporting the child's representation of Christ.

Now, we'll look at the woman who is with child. Besides being pregnant, there are some distinct features about her that reveal her true identity. It must be made adamantly clear that the woman is not Mary, Jesus' earthly mother, who is mistakenly deified by the Catholic Church.

Again, using scriptures to interpret itself, we go to Genesis 37:8–9 which provides a similar description which came from a dream that one of the sons of Jacob, Joseph, was given. In this passage of the Scripture, Joseph is telling his family of his dreams. When he was telling the second dream to his brothers and parents, he relayed that the sun, moon, and 11 stars were bowing down to him. He is sharply rebuked by his father because the symbolism of the sun, moon, and stars related to his father, mother (Rachel), and 11 brothers, not counting Joseph himself.

In regard to the woman, or the moon, there are scriptures that refer to the nation of Israel as a woman, such as Jeremiah 3:8: "I gave faithless Israel her certificate of divorce and sent her away because of all her adulteries. Yet I saw that her unfaithful sister Judah had no fear; she also went out and committed adultery."

So proven by the scriptures, we have an interpretation that clearly fits—a woman clothed with the sun, the moon under her feet, and 12 stars upon her head represents the nation of Israel and the 12 tribes of Israel or from Jacob.

Now, we have more confirmation that the child is Jesus, since Christ is a Jew from the lineage of Jacob, and was birthed by the nation of Israel to save them.

Moving on to verse 3, there is another sign of a great red dragon with seven heads, ten horns, and seven diadems (or crowns) on his head. This one is simpler to decipher since we know that the dragon is the serpent of old or Satan.

We can be sure of the fact that as the dragon was symbolic of Satan, the tail sweeping a third of the stars from heaven to earth is also symbolic.

- Previous texts in Revelation have proven the use of fallen stars to represent fallen angels.
- We also know that Satan (the dragon) led a rebellion in heaven and convinced one third of the angels in heaven to follow him. In essence, they were "swept" out of heaven by the devil's influence.

The next sign is the dragon's detailed description of seven heads, ten horns, and seven crowns. For more clarity, we'll go to Daniel 7:7–8 which speaks of the final Gentile kingdom. This kingdom was said to be different from the other kingdoms and had 10 horns, which represent leaders.

- These 10 kings are further represented as toes on the statue in Daniel 2.
- They are represented as the 10 horns described on the beast in Daniel 7.

So here, we have an interpretation of the sign:

- As we know, the dragon is Satan.
- The seven heads are the leaders under his control.
- The 10 horns are 10 kingdoms ruled by those leaders.
- And Satan, who is the god of this world, is pulling the strings of everyone.

In addition, we read in verse 4 that after sweeping one third of the stars down to earth with him, the dragon is poised to stand before the woman who is about to give birth in order to devour her child immediately after he is born. So now the picture comes more into view that the dragon, who is Satan, has plotted and schemed ever since the fall of man to corrupt the bloodline from which the Messiah would come.

Because after the fall, the prophecy was given in Genesis 3:15 that the Lord would put enmity between Satan and the woman and between his seed and her seed, and her seed would eventually crush the seed of the serpent. Christ, who is God's chosen vessel, was meant to be born through a woman.

That is why throughout Bible history, we can find numerous times when the enemy has fought against the woman in an attempt to abort the birth of the promised one, Jesus Christ—from the death of Abel at the hands of Cain, to the death of the firstborn males by Pharaoh on Egypt, to king Herod's murder of the children after the birth of Jesus. But despite his many attempts, God's plan of salvation was manifested through the birth of Jesus Christ.

This would put Satan on a time clock before his kingdom was no more, and Christ's kingdom would be established where He would rule with a rod of iron.

Revelation 12:6 Revealed

Revelation 12:6 lets us know that the woman fled into the wilderness from the presence of the dragon to a place that was prepared by God for her. She is to be nourished in the wilderness for 1,260 days, a number we're familiar with, that calculates to three and a half years. We know by now that this points to the mid-tribulation. We're not told about the specification of where the wilderness will be, but we can determine that the nation of Israel will be taken care of by God for the latter three and a half years of the tribulation.

Revelation 12:7–12 Revealed

Straight after, we enter a scene of war where Michael the archangel and his angels are fighting against the dragon, or Satan, and his angels. This war is different from the original banishment of Satan from heaven because of the period in time it is happening, which is during mid-tribulation. And we'll evidence of that in the coming verses.

We're told in verses 8–9 that Satan and his angels were not strong enough and no longer had access to God's throne. He was thrown to the earth along with his angels. Up until that time, Satan had access back and forth to God's throne where he accused believers before God, as was the case in Job 1:6–7:

> One day the angels came to present themselves before the LORD, and Satan also came with them. The LORD said to Satan, "Where have you come from?" Satan answered the LORD, "From roaming throughout the earth, going back and forth on it."

Now that Satan no longer has access to heaven, he will not be as powerful as he once was. There follows a celebration and declaration of his expulsion from heaven and the coming authority and rulership of Christ, because those in heaven know that Satan has long been accusing the believers before God's throne day and night.

However, despite his accusations against God's people, verse 11 shows us that we overcame Satan by the blood of the Lamb and by our testimonies and the sold-out followers in Jesus Christ. Even now, this is how believers are enduring Satan's attacks.

Revelation 12:12 warns of woe coming to the earth and the sea now that the devil has been cast down and confined to that environment. With no access to heaven, Satan understands that his rulership on earth will also be ending soon. That is why we are told that he has a short time. Because of time constraints, he is full of anger and wrath, especially against those who are believers during the three and a half years left of tribulation. Martyrdom and persecution will increase exponentially during this period.

Some may question why God didn't restrict Satan's access to heaven much sooner. But we must understand that God's timing is perfect. The earth and its inhabitants must only endure Satan's wrath for three and a half years. If he were cast down sooner, he would've caused much more damage. This is also in reference to Matthew 24:22 where Jesus is talking about the last days: "If those days had not been cut short, no one would survive, but for the sake of the elect those days will be shortened."

We'll get a display of Satan's unbridled wrath in the next few verses.

Revelation 12:13–16 Revealed

Once Satan realizes he has been cast to earth, he immediately attacks and persecutes the woman who gave birth to the child—Israel. There are very infamous names in history known for attacking the Jewish people, but we'll see that as a means of self-preservation, Satan persecutes the Jewish nation because it "gave birth" to Jesus Christ.

In response to his attacks, verse 14 shows us that the woman is given the wings of an eagle so she can be transported to the wilderness where she will be nourished for three and a half years. This is also to protect her from the devil's ruthless attacks. But just as the woman is symbolic of Israel, the eagle's wings can expect to be symbolic also.

In case you haven't been made aware, there are certain aspects of the Book of Revelation that mirror the Old Testament. The concept of being given two wings of an eagle to swoop the woman to safety isn't new, as we find in Exodus 19:3–4 which reads:

> Then Moses went up to God, and the LORD called to him from the mountain and said, "This is what you are to say to the descendants of Jacob and what you are to tell the people of Israel: 'You yourselves have seen what I did to Egypt, and how I carried you on eagles' wings and brought you to myself.

Here, God Himself is using the eagle's wings symbolically to describe the supernatural protection He gave His people in the wilderness after leaving Egypt. In like manner, the woman, who represents Israel, is also being transported to the wilderness by the great eagle in order to escape the dragon's persecution.

But the similarities to the story of Exodus doesn't stop here. In Revelation 12:15–16, the serpent is enraged at the woman's escape to the wilderness and belches out water from his mouth in an attempt to sweep the woman away with a flood. But because of God's protection, the earth helps her by swallowing up the raging river of water that the serpent sent to destroy her.

This all sounds remarkably similar to the way Pharaoh and his army chased down the Israelites after they left Egypt and were crossing over the Red Sea. In that scene, the Red Sea opened miraculously for the Israelites to cross over but swallowed Pharaoh and his army when they attempted the same. The "eagle's wings" can be seen as the earth supernaturally opening the Red Sea for the Israelites, while further helping them by drowning their pursuers.

Realizing his failure to consume the woman, the dragon is even more enraged and goes to make war with the rest of her children who keep the commandments of God and testify of Jesus Christ. Being that we know the "woman" in Chapter 12 is the nation of Israel, it would make sense that her children are the Jewish people. However, some Jews keep the commandments of God, or the laws of Moses, but don't believe in the Messiah.

But Satan's vendetta isn't only with the offspring of Israel but also with anyone who holds faith in Jesus Christ. So that means believing Gentiles are also targets in his radar. Essentially, Satan's war is against unbelieving Jews and believing Gentiles. Heading deeper into the second half of the tribulation, these two groups will be persecuted, hunted, and martyred by Satan.

End-of-Chapter Quiz

1. Who does the woman symbolize in verse 1?
2. Who is the male child the woman is pregnant with?
3. Who is the red dragon with seven heads, ten horns, and seven crowns?
4. Who cast Satan out of heaven?
5. Why does Satan go to attack the woman's offspring who keep the commandments of God?

Answers

1. Judging from the symbolism, the woman represents the nation of Israel, and the 12 stars on her head represent the 12 tribes of Israel.

2. The child is Jesus since we're told that he was caught up to God's throne.
3. The red dragon is meant to symbolize Satan and the kingdoms and leaders under his control.
4. Michael the archangel and his angels cast down Satan to earth with his fallen angels.
5. Satan knows that it won't be long before he is finally judged after being cast out of heaven. So in order to stop Christ's coming, he wants to wipe out the Jews and believers in God.

13

REVELATION 13—THE BEAST FROM THE SEA AND FROM THE EARTH

REVELATION 13:1–18

The Beast out of the Sea

The dragon stood on the shore of the sea. And I saw a beast coming out of the sea. It had ten horns and seven heads, with ten crowns on its horns, and on each head a blasphemous name. The beast I saw resembled a leopard, but had feet like those of a bear and a mouth like that of a lion. The dragon gave the beast his power and his throne and great authority. One of the heads of the beast seemed to have had a fatal wound, but the fatal wound had been healed. The whole world was filled with wonder and followed the beast. People worshiped the dragon because he had given authority to the beast, and they also worshiped the beast and asked, "Who is like the beast? Who can wage war against it?" The beast was given a mouth to utter proud words and blasphemies and to exercise its authority for forty-two months. It opened its mouth to blaspheme God, and to slander his name and his dwelling place and those who live in heaven. It was given power to wage war against God's holy people and to conquer them. And it was given authority over every tribe, people, language and nation. All inhabitants of the earth will worship the beast—all whose names have not been written in the Lamb's book of life, the Lamb who was slain from the creation of the world. Whoever has ears, let them hear. "If anyone is to go into captivity, into captivity they will go. If anyone is to be killed with the sword, with the sword they will be killed." This calls for patient endurance and faithfulness on the part of God's people.

The Beast out of the Earth

Then I saw a second beast, coming out of the earth. It had two horns like a lamb, but it spoke like a dragon. It exercised all the authority of the first beast on its behalf, and made the earth and its inhabitants worship the first beast, whose fatal wound had been healed. And it performed great signs, even causing fire to come down from heaven to the earth in full view of the people. Because of the signs it was given power to perform on behalf of the first beast, it deceived the inhabitants of the earth. It ordered them to set up an image in honor of the beast who was wounded by the sword and yet lived. The second beast was given power to give breath to the image of the first beast, so that the image could speak and cause all who refused to worship the image to be killed. It also forced all people, great and small, rich and poor, free and slave, to receive a mark on

> their right hands or on their foreheads, so that they could not buy or sell unless they had the mark, which is the name of the beast or the number of its name. This calls for wisdom. Let the person who has insight calculate the number of the beast, for it is the number of a man. That number is 666.

Revelation 13:1–2 Revealed

We last left off in Chapter 12 with the dragon, or Satan, losing his access to heaven and being banished to the earth with one third of his fallen angels. He is extremely angry with his new confinement, and those who live on the earth and in the sea are put on alert because of his great wrath. He is especially infuriated with the nation of Israel, her children (the Jewish people), and anyone who has put their faith in Jesus Christ. Let's see what awaits in the second half of the tribulation in Revelation 13.

In the opening verse of Revelation 13, we're given the imagery of the dragon on the seashore. Then we are introduced to a familiar character called the beast who is coming up from the sea. The characteristics of the beast are also familiar, being that it has ten horns, seven heads, and ten crowns on those heads. We can be sure that this is the dragon spoken of in Chapter 12 verse 3, which is Satan himself. But instead of being called the dragon in this passage, he is called a beast.

Also, if you remember, the word "beast" was also used in Chapter 11 verse 7 to describe the demonic power that came from the abyss to kill the two witnesses at mid-tribulation. We've already decoded that the original dragon with ten horns, seven heads, and ten crowns are political systems and kingdoms of men that have risen throughout the ages. Therefore, the beast rising out of the sea also represents nations, leaders, and political systems.

In the same way that Jesus uses believers in the body of Christ to do good works, so does Satan operate through people on earth to accomplish his agenda. The beast has been present throughout the book of Revelation, albeit in other forms, such as the rider of all four horsemen of the Apocalypse. It will be made known that the beast, who is beginning to take center stage, is actually the Antichrist.

We also have more symbolism in regard to the beast rising from the sea. What does the sea represent? The answer to that can be found in Daniel 7, which mirrors the text in Revelation 13:1 of a beast coming from the sea. The word "sea" in Daniel 7 referred to a Gentile nation, and we are also told that four beasts emerged from the sea. So the beast will be coming out of a Gentile nation, given power by the dragon or Satan.

John tells us in Revelation 13:2 that the beast was like a leopard, had the feet of a bear, and had the mouth of a lion. Sounds like a gene-spliced mutation, right? But this blasphemous creature depicted in Daniel 7:4–8 also fits the description in Revelation 13:2. Each beast in Daniel represents a dominating world power:

- the lion represented Babylon
- the bear represented Medo-Persia
- the leopard represented Greece

It then becomes clear that the Revelation 13 beast is the culmination of the beasts spoken of in Daniel 7, the most powerful leader of the age of the Gentiles—the Antichrist! He will also be the leader of the fourth kingdom on earth, as mentioned in Daniel 7:23, which we are told will be different from the other kingdoms and will crush and devour the whole earth.

Verse 2 also informs us that the beast will be given its throne and authority by the dragon, or Satan, directly. Although the previous kingdoms were all influenced by Satan, they have never been directly powered by him or become as powerful as him. Just as Christ and the Father became one, the beast and Satan will also become one.

Revelation 13:3 Revealed

Then in verse 3, we're told that one of the heads of the beast receives a fatal head wound, which is later healed, causing the entire world to follow after the beast in amazement. As we know, the seven heads of the beast represent world leaders, the seventh of which is the Antichrist. A head being slain is akin to a leader dying, in this case the Antichrist, by something or someone at mid-tribulation. The word "fatal" in this context means the death of the body. Therefore, the Antichrist receives a wound that would appear to kill him physically but then is brought to life again.

The only way to accomplish such a miraculous resurrection would only be by supernatural means. We know that God has the power to restore life, but this isn't His resurrection power at work. Therefore, the Lord allows Satan to indwell the Antichrist and bring him back to life, which makes him even more powerful and admired in the sight of the world. And this admiration is expressed in the next verse.

Revelation 13:4 Revealed

It's no mystery that Satan has desired to be God and has desired to be worshiped like Him, which is what caused pride and envy to enter his heart from the beginning. So verse 4 shows us how his perceived miraculous resurrection causes the world to worship the beast and, by so doing, worship the dragon (Satan) that has possessed him. He is being worshiped like a god through the body of the Antichrist, which is how he becomes the ruler of the world at mid-tribulation.

We see that, although he hates Him, he longs to be like Jesus Christ who was risen from the dead by God's resurrection power. By attempting to take the place of Christ, he becomes an Antichrist or a counterfeit Christ.

Paul even confirms Satan's plot in 2 Thessalonians 2:3–4 which reads:

> Don't let anyone deceive you in any way, for that day will not come until the rebellion occurs and the man of lawlessness is revealed, the man doomed to destruction. He will oppose and will exalt himself over everything that is called God or is worshiped, so that he sets himself up in God's temple, proclaiming himself to be God.

We are warned of Satan's ambitions in Daniel 11:36–39 which tells us that he (the Antichrist) will exalt and magnify himself above every god and will speak proudly and contemptuously against the God of gods, the Almighty. Simply put, he will make himself to be worshiped as the Messiah and will put an end to the worship of any other god or religion on earth so that he (Satan) will receive all the praise.

Revelation 13:5–10 Revealed

Highlighting what we just mentioned in Daniel 11, Revelation 13:5 reiterates the fact that the Antichrist will speak proud blasphemies against the God of heaven, His name, and tabernacle for a period of 42 months or three and a half years. Obviously, with the world marveling after his resurrection, his declaration of being God leaves a profound impact on many in the world, who are deceived into believing his claims.

Remember when we mentioned in Chapter 12 that Satan declared war against the offspring of the woman? Well, he's showing his horns in verse 7 when it says that he was permitted to make war with the saints and overcome them. That shouldn't be surprising, since the believers are the only ones in the world who won't worship him as the true Messiah. As a result, they will be seen as disobedient, and the Antichrist will be allowed to overcome and kill them.

Verse 8 confirms to us that all the inhabitants of the earth whose names are not written in the Lamb's Book of Life will worship the beast. Those who will not worship the beast are the elect. This is the period in tribulation where a dividing line must be drawn in regard to worship. Even if someone identifies as a believer and begins to worship the beast, their names will be removed from the Book of Life. It will be a true test of faith for many believers who will have to choose whether to worship the beast and preserve their lives but be condemned or to faithfully worship Jesus and die to inherit eternal life.

John then gives a sobering reality in verse 10 of the fate many followers of Christ will have to face. Since the Antichrist will be in complete rulership by this time, if they refuse to give him their worship, they will die. This will be the life saints must endure for two and a half years under the Antichrist's reign. God's people are encouraged to persevere during this time, even if that means accepting the fate of martyrdom.

Revelation 13:11–14 Revealed

Now that we've covered the beast coming out of the sea, Revelation 13:11 introduces us to the beast from the earth. The symbolism of a lamb and a dragon is used to describe this beast, and of course, they have a symbolic meaning. Biblically, a lamb is used to describe Christ and His sacrificial ministry, which is why He is called the Lamb of God. The beast also has the mouth of a dragon, which stands for Satan.

The following verse tells us that he will exercise authority like the first beast, and his main function will be to cause those who dwell on earth to worship the first beast who is risen from the dead by Satan. The second beast is basically a false prophet who is a mouthpiece for the Antichrist who leads others to believe in his divinity.

As we were told in verse 12, the false prophet of tribulation will be operating from the power and authority of Satan, who indwells the first beast. This authority is put on display in verse 13 with lying signs and wonders, even causing fire to come down from heaven before men to further convince the world that the Antichrist is god. Since Satan is not God Almighty, he is not omniscient. Therefore, the false prophet must rely on Satan's power resting inside of the Antichrist in order to perform these signs and wonders.

As he is the spokesman and promoter for the Antichrist, verse 4 shows us that the false prophet commands an image of the Antichrist to be constructed. Adding insult to injury, having people worship the image of the beast is idolatry and is another trap of Satan to sneer souls. Sadly, many churches and false religions have erred by breaking this commandment from God.

Revelation 13:15–18 Revealed

What's more is that we're told the false prophet gave breath to the image of the beast, causing the image to speak and causing any that refused to worship the image to be killed. But what could make an image speak and breathe? Since we're dealing with the power of Satan, a demonically charged relic of the Antichrist would make sense.

Now that we've dealt with the worship through a spiritual lens, we'll look at how the Antichrist obtains worship through economic means. Revelation 13:16 tells us that he causes every human being on earth to receive a mark in their right hand or in their forehead in order to buy or sell anything. This is similar to the marking of the 144,000 bond servants of Christ in Chapter 7; only those with the Antichrist's mark are doomed to a fiery lake.

The Antichrist's mark is 666, which John tells us is the number of his name. His name is given a mathematical quantity due to a unique Jewish name-numbering method. It works by assigning a numerical value to each 22 characters of the Hebrew alphabet. Bear in mind that this only works with Hebrew names. So in order to arrive at 666, the Antichrist's name must also be written in Hebrew. Further confirming his identity, the number six in the Scripture is the number of the fallen man.

Also, in Hebrew writing, to double a number means "more," and tripling a number means "most." The number 666 is then fitting for the Antichrist, who is the most sinful man in history since Satan inhabits his body.

A lot has taken place in Chapter 13 to kick off the mid-tribulation. The events on the earth begin to intensify as Christ's return draws ever closer. A major cause of the increase of these events is Satan's fall to earth, which has brought with it all his wrath.

The false prophet is introduced to initiate mankind's worship of the Antichrist, who by default will be worshiping Satan since he indwells him. As the world marvels after the beast following his orchestrated death and resurrection, believers are persecuted because they refuse to worship the Antichrist as god or to bow down to his image.

Being the true counterfeit he is, Satan creates an economic system of worship where he forces the people of earth to take his mark to buy and sell. But in essence, he is only imitating what God did with the 144,000 sealed servants.

Let's see where Chapter 14 takes us next on our journey through the tribulation.

End-of-Chapter Quiz

1. Who is the beast from the sea?
2. Who is the beast from the earth?
3. How does the Antichrist make war with the saints and overcome them?
4. What is the 666 mark of the beast used for?
5. How else does the Antichrist cause people to worship him?

Answers

1. The beast from the sea represents nations, leaders, and political systems that have served Satan. The Antichrist will be the main political leader.
2. The beast from the earth is represented by the false prophet who will be the mouthpiece that leads many to worship the Antichrist.
3. Through lying signs and wonders, the Antichrist will appear to be godlike to the world and will demand worship. Those who don't submit will be martyred.
4. To further gain control over the nations, the Antichrist installs a new economic system that requires buyers and sellers to receive his mark, 666, on their hand or forehead.
5. The false prophet sets up an image of the Antichrist that will cause people to worship him.

14

REVELATION 14—THE PROCLAMATIONS OF THREE ANGELS

REVELATION 14:1–20

The Lamb and the 144,000

Then I looked, and there before me was the Lamb, standing on Mount Zion, and with him 144,000 who had his name and his Father's name written on their foreheads. And I heard a sound from heaven like the roar of rushing waters and like a loud peal of thunder. The sound I heard was like that of harpists playing their harps. And they sang a new song before the throne and before the four living creatures and the elders. No one could learn the song except the 144,000 who had been redeemed from the earth. These are those who did not defile themselves with women, for they remained virgins. They follow the Lamb wherever he goes. They were purchased from among mankind and offered as firstfruits to God and the Lamb. No lie was found in their mouths; they are blameless.

The Three Angels

Then I saw another angel flying in midair, and he had the eternal gospel to proclaim to those who live on the earth—to every nation, tribe, language and people. He said in a loud voice, "Fear God and give him glory, because the hour of his judgment has come. Worship him who made the heavens, the earth, the sea and the springs of water." A second angel followed and said, "'Fallen! Fallen is Babylon the Great,' which made all the nations drink the maddening wine of her adulteries." A third angel followed them and said in a loud voice: "If anyone worships the beast and its image and receives its mark on their forehead or on their hand, they, too, will drink the wine of God's fury, which has been poured full strength into the cup of his wrath. They will be tormented with burning sulfur in the presence of the holy angels and of the Lamb. And the smoke of their torment will rise for ever and ever. There will be no rest day or night for those who worship the beast and its image, or for anyone who receives the mark of its name." This calls for patient endurance on the part of the people of God who keep his commands and remain faithful to Jesus. Then I heard a voice from heaven say, "Write this: Blessed are the dead who die in the Lord from now on." "Yes," says the Spirit, "they will rest from their labor, for their deeds will follow them."

Harvesting the Earth and Trampling the Winepress

I looked, and there before me was a white cloud, and seated

> on the cloud was one like a son of man with a crown of gold on his head and a sharp sickle in his hand. Then another angel came out of the temple and called in a loud voice to him who was sitting on the cloud, "Take your sickle and reap, because the time to reap has come, for the harvest of the earth is ripe." So he who was seated on the cloud swung his sickle over the earth, and the earth was harvested. Another angel came out of the temple in heaven, and he too had a sharp sickle. Still another angel, who had charge of the fire, came from the altar and called in a loud voice to him who had the sharp sickle, "Take your sharp sickle and gather the clusters of grapes from the earth's vine, because its grapes are ripe." The angel swung his sickle on the earth, gathered its grapes and threw them into the great winepress of God's wrath. They were trampled in the winepress outside the city, and blood flowed out of the press, rising as high as the horses' bridles for a distance of 1,600 stadia.

Revelation 14:1 Revealed

Revelation 14 kicks off with John looking at a scene of the Lamb (Jesus Christ) who is standing on Mount Zion with 144,000 saints who have Christ's name and His Father's name written on their foreheads. By now, we know that the 144,000 are all Jewish men chosen and sealed by God, and here, they accompany Jesus on Mount Zion. However, we can't be sure that they are on Mount Zion in present-day Jerusalem. But it is ironic that after ending Chapter 13 going over the Antichrist's mark of 666 and those who receive it, the topic of the 144,000 is again being discussed. Since this is all we know, let's proceed to the next text.

Revelation 14:2–5 Revealed

John then hears a very unique voice from heaven which sounded more like the sound of thundering voices mixed with harpists playing their harps. Verse 3 lets us know that the voice from a song was being sung before the throne by the four living creatures and the 144,000.

We know that the 144,000 are singing because later in the verse we are told that no one could learn that song except the 144,000 who were standing with Christ on Mount Zion and had been "purchased from the earth." Being "purchased" means that they have been redeemed by the blood of Christ. Being purchased "from the earth" alludes to the fact that they were removed from earth and have now arrived in heaven.

In verses 4–5, we are told of some distinct characteristics of the 144,000:

- They were redeemed as firstfruits for God, which means that they were the best options to be harvested. Generally, when reaping and producing, the best fruit (low-hanging fruit) is harvested first. The law recognizes firstfruits as an offering of thanks unto God.
- They were the first group to receive and spread faith in Christ following the rapture.
- These men were not defiled with women, meaning they were completely devoted to following Christ.
- This is the reason we are told that they follow the Lamb wherever He goes. They were not distracted by the earthly

pleasure of marriage and were single-mindedly serving God.

- Finally, we are told in verse 5 that they are blameless because they never told a lie. While they were not sinless, it takes great faith and devotion to never speak a lie.

The 144,000 are unquestionably an exemplary model for obedient martyrdom in a time when the world is flooded with sin. It's for this reason that they are called the firstfruits to God. They are even removed before the worst of the tribulation begins and are among the first to bask in the glory with Christ in heaven.

Revelation 14:6–7 Revealed

For the second time in Revelation 14:6, John sees another angel flying in midheaven proclaiming an eternal gospel to all the people of the world. The last time he saw an angel flying in midheaven was to announce the woe judgments. The angel is said to be preaching the eternal gospel because it's the same message of salvation that has always been preached—that the only way to receive salvation is through Jesus Christ.

The angel beckons to the world to fear God and worship the Creator of heaven and earth because the hour of His judgment has come. In other words, he's saying time is short, the window of grace is closing, and it's time to clean the house. By saying the "hour" of God's judgment has come implies a short time. It's a reminder that the only person who needs to truly be feared is the Lord, not physical death, lack of resources, or the Antichrist.

Other than being the final declaration before earthly judgment, it's also a warning to convict the nations of the world so that everyone will be without excuse. Christ assured His followers in Matthew 24:14 that before the end comes, the gospel would be preached to every nation in the world: "And this gospel of the kingdom will be preached in the whole world as a testimony to all nations, and then the end will come."

Apart from the numerous Christian missionaries around the world, the angel's message of the gospel is proclaimed to the entire world in one moment, just as Jesus promised.

Revelation 14:8–11 Revealed

After the angel in verse 7 declares his warning to the earth, another angel follows with a warning addressed to the Antichrist's kingdom named Babylon. After he has been kicked out of heaven, it's now being announced by the angel that Babylon, the great, has fallen—and rightfully so, because she has made nations drunk with her immorality and whoredom. Although the original kingdom of Babylon was ruled by King Nebuchadnezzar since around 500 B.C.E., it represents the kingdom from which all other Antichrist archetype kingdoms stem from, leading up to the second half of the tribulation period.

In the next verse, a third angel loudly proclaims that anyone who worships the beast and his image or receives his mark will experience God's wrath and be tormented forever. He makes it clear that there will be no second chances for whoever submits to the Antichrist.

We're also told in verse 11 that the torment of those with the mark will be a ceaseless, slow burn that will engulf them day and night. They will suffer in the heat of fire and brimstone in the presence of the Lamb and the holy angels for choosing the temporary pleasures of sin over eternal life with Christ.

The topic of hell and eternal punishment seems taboo and hard to believe for many unbelievers and even some professing believers to grasp. The idea that a loving God would allow some of His creation to burn in torment indefinitely seems cruel. But God hates sin, especially when there is no repentance. So God's wrath and eternal judgment is the punishment for a willingly sinful nature.

Revelation 14:12–13 Revealed

Verse 12 begins and it's not another angel this time; John is pointing out that here is where the perseverance of the saints is required to remain hopeful during the last three and a half years of tribulation.

Then we hear a voice from heaven speak saying that those who die in the Lord early on are blessed. In a world as sinful and hateful as the one at that time, dying is seen as more of a blessing. They are set free from the limitation of their earthly bodies and can rest from the fear of persecution from the enemy. Their deeds also follow them into the afterlife, which comes with eternal rewards for the saints who persevere during trials here on earth, such as a new glorified body and everlasting life in the kingdom.

Revelation 14:14–16 Revealed

The judgment of Babylon is also a time of reaping, and we see that in Revelation 14:14 when one like the "son of man" holding a sharp sickle in his hand and sitting on a cloud is told by an angel to put in his sickle and reap because the harvest of the earth is ripe. While John doesn't say plainly who the "son of man" holding the sickle is, since the term is reserved as a messianic term in the New Testament, we can suspect it to be Christ. But it's unlikely that Christ will take an order from an angel in His glorified state, so we assume the figure riding on the cloud with the sickle to be another angel.

But what is the angel reaping? Similar to the first ripe fruits that were reaped (the 144,000 tribulation saints), the angel is reaping the souls of believers through martyrdom. So as the saints are being killed at the hands of the Antichrist, they are being regathered as the elect for Jesus' Second Coming.

Revelation 14:17–20 Revealed

We are given confirmation of this time of harvesting in verse 17 as we're told of another angel coming out of heaven with a sharp sickle. He is told by another angel with power over fire to put in his sickle and gather clusters from the vine of the earth because her grapes are ripe. However, this angel is harvesting a different group from the earth. There is a reaping of the believers and the unbelievers, and the latter is to be thrown in the winepress of the great wrath of God.

Being placed into the winepress of God's wrath brings about great bloodshed and is referencing the war of Armageddon at the end of the mid-tribulation period. The last verse even tells us that the blood from the winepress was as high as the horses' bridles and ran for a distance of 200 miles. The average height of a horse bridle is four and a half feet, which, coupled with the 200-mile distance, is the measurement of a ravine in Israel. This is a mere description of the blood that will flow from the armies who battle in the valley of Kidron for the final battle at the end of tribulation.

The End of Trumpet Judgments and the Start of Bowl Judgments

The end of Chapter 14 marks the culmination of the trumpet judgments, and the coming chapters will usher into the end of tribulation. We've been shown the dread and terror that awaits the unbelievers who receive the mark of the beast and worship the image of the Antichrist and get a sneak preview of the police state persecution that nonconformists will have to endure, particularly Christians and Jews. Coming up are the seven plagues and the seven bowl judgments that must take place.

End-of-Chapter Quiz

1. Who is standing on Mount Zion with Christ in verse 1?
2. What does it mean that the 144,000 were "purchased from the earth"?
3. What happens to the people who received the mark of the beast?
4. Why is Babylon going to be judged?

Answers

1. The 144,000 are standing with Christ with God's seal in their foreheads.
2. Being "purchased from the earth" means that the 144,000 have been bought with the blood of Christ and have been taken from earth to heaven.
3. We're told in verse 11 that those who receive the mark of the beast will be tormented for eternity in the lake of fire.
4. Babylon is the spiritual power working with the Antichrist to further his plan for worldwide worship. Spiritual Babylon has gotten the nations of the world drunk from her immorality and spiritual wickedness.

15

REVELATION 15—SEVEN ANGELS WITH SEVEN PLAGUES

REVELATION 15:1–8

Seven Angels With Seven Plagues

I saw in heaven another great and marvelous sign: seven angels with the seven last plagues—last, because with them God's wrath is completed. And I saw what looked like a sea of glass glowing with fire and, standing beside the sea, those who had been victorious over the beast and its image and over the number of its name. They held harps given them by God and sang the song of God's servant Moses and of the Lamb: "Great and marvelous are your deeds, Lord God Almighty. Just and true are your ways, King of the nations. Who will not fear you, Lord, and bring glory to your name? For you alone are holy. All nations will come and worship before you, for your righteous acts have been revealed." After this I looked, and I saw in heaven the temple—that is,

> the tabernacle of the covenant law—and it was opened. Out of the temple came the seven angels with the seven plagues. They were dressed in clean, shining linen and wore golden sashes around their chests. Then one of the four living creatures gave to the seven angels seven golden bowls filled with the wrath of God, who lives for ever and ever. And the temple was filled with smoke from the glory of God and from his power, and no one could enter the temple until the seven plagues of the seven angels were completed.

Revelation 15:1 Revealed

We've officially entered the final quarter, or rather the final half, of the tribulation. In Revelation 15:1, John's attention is again drawn to heaven where he sees seven angels who hold the seven last plagues which are the last judgments of tribulation, also known as the bowl judgments.

And according to the final seven-year period spoken of in the Book of Daniel, the bowl judgments are a part of the Old Covenant between the Lord and Israel. This is expressed in Daniel 9:24 which reads:

> Seventy 'sevens' are decreed for your people and your holy city to finish transgression, to put an end to sin, to atone for wickedness, to bring in everlasting righteousness, to seal up vision and prophecy and to anoint the Most Holy Place.

Therefore, the wrath being poured out on Israel during the final seven years of tribulation is in keeping with the agreement to make an end to their sin of unbelief. The Jews, who Christ came to earth to redeem back to the Father, were the very ones who rejected and crucified Him. So for the remainder of the tribulation period, Israel will be the centerpiece of God's judgment which will cause the unbelieving Jews to perish while the refining process will bring others to faith in Christ. Additionally, he will be bringing judgment on an unbelieving world by means of a judgment that has been long overdue.

Revelation 15:2–4 Revealed

Continuing with John's heavenly vision in verse 2, he tries to explain the fantastical features in heaven by combining the elements on earth and stating that he saw a sea of glass mixed with fire, although that's hard to believe. We can appreciate John's effort to relay his visions through imagery since there aren't many references in his time to describe what he saw.

Standing on the sea of glass, he sees the believers who were victorious over the beast, meaning that they chose martyrdom in the tribulation over submission to the beast, his image, and his mark. They have left the world dominated by the enemy and didn't love their physical lives more than they loved the Lord, having passed the biggest test any believer will face during the tribulation.

Revelation 15:3 paints a picture of their victorious celebration as they sing the song of Moses and the song of the Lamb while playing harps. The song is recorded in verse 3 and gives praise to Jesus, who they call the Lamb, as the righteous King of nations. The choir of saints is already declaring that all nations will worship before Jesus once His righteous acts have been revealed for the world to see. The declarations inform us that the tribulation is coming to a close and the Second Coming of Jesus is very near.

We mentioned in verse 3 that in addition to the song of the Lamb, the saints also sang the song of Moses, which can be found in Deuteronomy 32:5–41. As its name suggests, the song is written by Moses just before he dies and the Israelites enter into the promised land. Throughout the time that Moses led the Israelites out of Egypt, most of them have grieved him and God because of their stubbornness and faithlessness. And the song highlights those aspects and the fact that they have worshiped other gods while rebelling against the one true God who saved them.

As a result, the Lord brings calamities upon His people with the intention to bring them low and break their rebellious, stubborn hearts. Moses' song is clearly prophetic, and the fulfillment of its content is seen at the end of tribulation, which is why it is introduced.

God established His relationship with Israel upon covenants—the Abrahamic and Mosaic covenants. The Abrahamic covenant was based on Israel's relationship with God and came without conditions. But there were conditions under the Mosaic covenant.

These conditions came as a result of Israel's disobedience, which resulted in the outpour of God's judgment for their sins in a period we know as the age of the Gentiles. And as we've learned, the age of the Gentiles culminates at the end of the tribulation.

Revelation 15:5 Revealed

We revert back to John's vision of the temple in heaven being opened, similar in fashion to the temple that God instructed Moses to build for Israel in the Old Testament law. We're also told in Hebrew 9:23–24 that the earthly tabernacle is built after the fashion of the heavenly tabernacle. The ark in the earthly tabernacle had a mercy seat, which is at the top of the ark. Here is where the Schechinah glory of God dwelled.

However, since the age of the Gentiles began, the glory of the Lord hasn't returned to Israel. The glory will only return when the kingdom of God is established on earth and a new temple is built.

However, since the age of the Gentiles began, the glory of the Lord hasn't returned to Israel. The glory will only return when the kingdom of God is established on earth and a new temple is built. With the Lord now pouring out the final bowls of His wrath on Israel and the world, the tabernacle in heaven opens up a sign that His glory will soon be returning to earth and will be dwelling with Israel.

Revelation 15:6–7 Revealed

With the preparation already made with the opening of the heavenly tabernacle, it's time for the seven angels to pour out the seven last plagues, which are the seven golden bowls of wrath. But before God's wrath can be poured out, the seventh trumpet will sound.

Throughout scriptures, God's wrath is seen as being stored or filled up in a cup, bowl, or other vessel. The bigger the vessel, the more severe the wrath will be. So as Israel has stored up seven bowls of wrath for herself, including that of the rest of the world, the judgment can be expected to be the worst we have seen.

The wrath of God is even expressed in Romans 2:5–6 which reads:

> But because of your stubbornness and your unrepentant heart, you are storing up wrath against yourself for the day of God's wrath, when his righteous judgment will be revealed. God "will repay each person according to what they have done."

The chapter concludes with the temple being filled with smoke which represents the glory and power of God. No one was allowed to enter into the temple filled with smoke until the seven plagues of the seven angels were poured out.

This is also the way the temple works on earth. In the holy of holies where the ark and the mercy seat were kept, only the high priest was allowed to enter. But since everyone has been prohibited from entering the temple while the bowls of wrath are poured out, which includes Jesus, our high priest, that means he cannot go to make intercession before the Father. And if Christ makes no intercession, there is no grace to be offered. Simply put, the wrath poured out from the seven bowls is final.

As we are being transitioned out of the mid-tribulation period, the final weeks will now be covered in Chapter 16.

End-of-Chapter Quiz

1. Who is standing on the sea of glass glowing with fire described by John?
2. Where can the original song of Moses be found that the believers are singing?
3. In what way was the song of Moses prophetic to the Book of Revelation?
4. Why couldn't anyone enter the temple in heaven until the bowls of wrath were poured out?

Answers

1. The believers who did not receive the mark of the beast and were victorious over the beast and his image.
2. The song of Moses can be found in Deuteronomy 32:5–41.
3. The song of Moses can be applied to the Book of Revelation because the reason the age of the Gentiles began was because of Israel's rebellion to God, similar to the rebellion of the Israelites in the wilderness with Moses.
4. In the tabernacle on earth, only the high priest was allowed to enter the holy of holies to make intercession for sin. In heaven, Christ is the high priest, and so He was prohibited from making intercession in the temple while the bowls of wrath were being poured out.

16

REVELATION 16—THE SEVEN BOWLS OF JUDGMENT

REVELATION 16:1–21

The Seven Bowls of God's Wrath

Then I heard a loud voice from the temple saying to the seven angels, "Go, pour out the seven bowls of God's wrath on the earth." The first angel went and poured out his bowl on the land, and ugly, festering sores broke out on the people who had the mark of the beast and worshiped its image. The second angel poured out his bowl on the sea, and it turned into blood like that of a dead person, and every living thing in the sea died. The third angel poured out his bowl on the rivers and springs of water, and they became blood. Then I heard the angel in charge of the waters say: "You are just in these judgments, O Holy One, you who are and who were; for they have shed the blood of your holy people and your prophets, and you have given them blood to drink as they deserve." And I heard the altar respond: "Yes, Lord God Almighty, true and just are your judgments." The fourth angel poured out his bowl on the sun, and the sun was allowed to scorch people with fire. They were seared by the intense heat and they cursed the name of God, who had control over these plagues, but they refused to repent and glorify him. The fifth angel poured out his bowl on the throne of the beast, and its kingdom was plunged into darkness. People gnawed their tongues in agony and cursed the God of heaven because of their pains and their sores, but they refused to repent of what they had done. The sixth angel poured out his bowl on the great river Euphrates, and its water was dried up to prepare the way for the kings from the East. Then I saw three impure spirits that looked like frogs; they came out of the mouth of the dragon, out of the mouth of the beast and out of the mouth of the false prophet. They are demonic spirits that perform signs, and they go out to the kings of the whole world, to gather them for the battle on the great day of God Almighty. "Look, I come like a thief! Blessed is the one who stays awake and remains clothed, so as not to go naked and be shamefully exposed." Then they gathered the kings together to the place that in Hebrew is called Armageddon. The seventh angel poured out his bowl into the air, and out of the temple came a loud voice from the throne, saying, "It is done!" Then there came flashes of lightning, rumblings, peals of thunder and a severe earthquake. No earthquake like it has ever occurred since mankind has been on earth, so tremendous was the quake. The great city split into three

> parts, and the cities of the nations collapsed. God remembered Babylon the Great and gave her the cup filled with the wine of the fury of his wrath. Every island fled away and the mountains could not be found. From the sky huge hailstones, each weighing about a hundred pounds, fell on people. And they cursed God on account of the plague of hail, because the plague was so terrible.

Revelation 16:1–11 Revealed

As promised, the bowl judgments will be even more severe and terrible than the previous judgments. Chapter 16 begins with a loud voice from the temple instructing the seven angels to pour out the seven bowls of wrath upon the earth.

- Shortly after, the first angel poured out his bowl, and a loathsome and wickedly painful sore came up on those with the mark of the beast who also worshiped the beast's image. The actual word used in the scripture to define the sore is malignant, which in Greek is the literal word for evil or wicked.
- The second angel poured his bowl into the sea, turning it like the blood of a dead man. The metaphor used to describe the blood was fitting because this bowl also caused every living thing in the sea to die. Realistically, the loss of marine life on such a grand scale would raise a foul stench from the blood of the dead fish in addition to causing an environmental disaster from a shutdown of the planet's water cycle.

- Adding insult to injury, the third angel poured out his bowl on the freshwater sources like rivers and springs, also turning them blood red. Then the angel praises the Lord for His righteous judgment and explains that the blood of these judgments is recompense on the world for the innocent blood of the saints that has been shed. Mankind won't be able to survive very long without drinking fresh water from a clean water source.
- In Revelation 16:8, the fourth angel poured his bowl out onto the sun, triggering to increase its output of solar energy to the degree that it scorches men's skin, literally! The combined events of the bowl judgments would turn earth into a living hell—numerous bloody, contaminated, dead fish-infested water sources, no production of rain (because the water has become blood), plus intensified heat from the sun causing the rapid decomposition of dead fish and a wretched stench in the air. The unbelievers would be getting a preview of what a burning hell is like.
- When the fifth angel poured out his bowl on the throne of the beast, it plunged the earth into darkness. But this isn't merely a darkness with no physical light. This is a spiritual darkness that befalls the kingdom of the beast and the earth, which causes unbearable pain. Just as Christ suffered pain on the cross and was abandoned by the Father, the world will also be left exposed to the forces of darkness as God removes His hand of protection and His presence from the earth.
- We read in verse 11 that, even with the severity of the bowl judgments, those who suffered through it refused to repent

of their deeds. Instead, they blasphemed the God of heaven even more because of the sores and pains they experienced, which only solidified their spot in the lake of fire.

Revelation 16:12–16 Revealed

Now that we've gotten through what can be considered the worst of the bowl judgments, we can proceed to Chapter 16 which covers the final two bowl judgments. We'll also discover how the bowl judgments relate to the war of Armageddon, especially the final two bowls. With that said, let's dive into Revelation 16:12:

- The chapter continues with the sixth angel pouring out his bowl in the Euphrates River, which subsequently dries its water. Although the river would've already turned to blood from the fifth angel's bowl judgment previously, it was purposely "dried up" in order to prepare a way for the kings of the east. This is a reference to the Antichrist and the seven kings he rules over during his reign on earth.
- Verse 13 shows us that out of the mouth of the dragon, the beast, and the false prophet came three unclean spirits like frogs which were sent to the kings of the earth to gather them together in the war of the great day of God Almighty. It's already been confirmed that the dragon, the beast, the and false prophet are by nature evil entities. An unclean spirit denotes a demon, and frogs are an Old Testament symbol for an unclean spirit. These demons are sent as messengers to gather the seven kings and their military forces to prepare for war against God.

- Verse 16 reveals that the name of the place where they gathered is Har-Megiddo. When broken down, the word *har* in Hebrew means hill or mountain, and Megiddo is a city in northern Israel in the Jezreel Valley, hence the word Har-Megiddo, which when translated in English is Armageddon.
- Finally, verse 15 inserts a reminder that Christ is coming like a thief, and only those believers who are expecting His coming and keep their garments on will be taken into heaven. Those who are walking "naked," or who are unbelievers, will be caught unaware at Jesus' Second Coming.

Why Wage War Against God?

You may have wondered to yourself why Satan would be so delusional to think he could wage war against God and win. But, like a scared dog backed into a corner, he's lashing out in a last ditch attempt to escape his fate, which is the lake of fire. After Satan's confinement to earth and the five terrible bowl judgments that followed, the world has been rendered virtually uninhabitable. Let's not forget that the once glorified cherub is scouring for a way to avoid death, as he knows his time is short.

Therefore, as a last resort, Satan uses the influence of the Antichrist and the false prophet to unite and join forces in confederacy with the world to wage war against Christ. It's for this reason that Satan gathers the armies of the seven kings to northern Israel so that they can attack the Lord's city, kill the Jews, and position themselves to attack Christ as He returns on the Mount of Olives.

But we know how the story ends. Christ will return with myriads of His holy ones and lay waste to their armies. The most important thing is to accept Christ today while there is time because tomorrow isn't promised. So the least anyone can do is prepare while there is yet time.

End-of-Chapter Quiz

1. What happened to those who received the mark of the beast after the first bowl was poured out?
2. What will happen to mankind after the marine life dies from the second bowl judgment?
3. What happened to the kingdom of the beast when the fifth angel poured out his bowl upon it?
4. What happened to the Euphrates River when the sixth angel poured out his bowl, and why is it significant?
5. What does it mean that we should remain clothed so as to not walk naked and be exposed?

Answers

1. We are told in verse 2 that a loathsome and painful sore broke out on the people who received the mark of the beast.
2. The death of marine life will cause environmental disasters like drought and crop failure.
3. The kingdom of the beast was plunged into deep spiritual darkness and was left exposed to dark demonic forces.

4. After the sixth angel poured out his bowl, the Euphrates River dried up, which prepared the way for the kings of the east serving the Antichrist to attack Israel.
5. A believer is clothed in Christ when he accepts Jesus as his Lord and Savior. To walk naked and be exposed means that you are not covered by Christ and are spiritually in danger.

17

REVELATION 17—THE SCARLET WOMAN AND THE BEAST

REVELATION 17:1–18

Babylon, the Prostitute on the Beast

One of the seven angels who had the seven bowls came and said to me, "Come, I will show you the punishment of the great prostitute, who sits by many waters. With her the kings of the earth committed adultery, and the inhabitants of the earth were intoxicated with the wine of her adulteries." Then the angel carried me away in the Spirit into a wilderness. There I saw a woman sitting on a scarlet beast that was covered with blasphemous names and had seven heads and ten horns. The woman was dressed in purple and scarlet, and was glittering with gold, precious stones and pearls. She held a golden cup in her hand, filled with abominable things and the filth of her adulteries. The name written on her forehead was a mystery: BABYLON THE GREAT THE

MOTHER OF PROSTITUTES AND OF THE ABOMINATIONS OF THE EARTH. I saw that the woman was drunk with the blood of God's holy people, the blood of those who bore testimony to Jesus. When I saw her, I was greatly astonished. Then the angel said to me: "Why are you astonished? I will explain to you the mystery of the woman and of the beast she rides, which has the seven heads and ten horns. The beast, which you saw, once was, now is not, and yet will come up out of the Abyss and go to its destruction. The inhabitants of the earth whose names have not been written in the book of life from the creation of the world will be astonished when they see the beast, because it once was, now is not, and yet will come. "This calls for a mind with wisdom. The seven heads are seven hills on which the woman sits. They are also seven kings. Five have fallen, one is, the other has not yet come; but when he does come, he must remain for only a little while. The beast who once was, and now is not, is an eighth king. He belongs to the seven and is going to his destruction. "The ten horns you saw are ten kings who have not yet received a kingdom, but who for one hour will receive authority as kings along with the beast. They have one purpose and will give their power and authority to the beast. They will wage war against the Lamb, but the Lamb will triumph over them because he is Lord of lords and King of kings—and with him will be his called, chosen and faithful followers." Then the angel said to me, "The waters you saw, where the prostitute sits, are peoples, multitudes, nations and languages. The beast and the ten horns you saw will hate the prostitute. They will bring her to ruin and leave her naked; they will eat

> her flesh and burn her with fire. For God has put it into their hearts to accomplish his purpose by agreeing to hand over to the beast their royal authority, until God's words are fulfilled. The woman you saw is the great city that rules over the kings of the earth."

Revelation 17:1–8 Revealed

We left off in Chapter 16 with the sixth bowl of wrath being poured out in preparation for the kings of the earth to be assembled for the battle of Armageddon. But before the war ensues, Revelation 17 will highlight a harlot known as Babylon, which we know to be the city once ruled by King Nebuchadnezzar. But as we read in verse 1, one of the seven angels is speaking to John about the judgment of the great harlot who sits on many waters and has committed acts of immorality with the kings of the earth. We can find some familiar symbolism in this verse.

- A harlot is known as a sexually immoral woman, a prostitute, or a counterfeit wife. In the Scripture, women are often used to symbolize religious systems. So by using a harlot to describe spiritual Babylon, it's being communicated to us that it's a false religion.
- In verse 2, the harlot's reputation is confirmed as we're told that she has made the kings of the earth drunk with the wine of her immorality, causing them to join her in acting immorally.
- We're also told that she sits on many "waters," which biblically represents multitudes of nations, peoples, and tongues worldwide. By saying that the great harlot sits on

many waters means that the deception of false religion is dominating over the world.

- We've been introduced to this beast in Revelation 13:1 with the same description. You can find this text in Chapter 13. If you remember, we discovered this beast to be the Antichrist who resurrected after a deadly head wound and is being praised by the world.
- Now we can see the diabolical plan of Satan, who is indwelling the Antichrist, to become one with the great whore of spiritual Babylon by allowing her to ride him. With their influences combined, the world will no longer be divided with many false religions but will now only serve the beast through a one world religion.
- Verse 4 tells us that the harlot spiritual system is adorned in purple and scarlet and is lavished in precious metals and jewels. She is also holding a gold cup, or chalice, filled with abomination and immorality that she indulges in.
- We find out in verse 6 what fills the cup of the harlot; she is drunk on the blood of the saints. This includes not only the martyred tribulation saints but also those throughout history who were witnesses of Jesus, which lets us know that Babylon the Great, the mother of harlots, has been around for centuries.
- False religions have been used as Satan's tool over the centuries to bring people into sin and lead them to hell. The most dangerous examples are those that use the name of Jesus under false pretense while persecuting the true believers in Christ.
- We're reminded in verse 8 who the beast is that carries the mother of harlots, that he is the one who was, and is not,

and is about to come up out of the abyss to go to destruction, referring to his orchestrated death and resurrection. This deceptive miracle will cause the world to marvel after the beast but only those whose names are not written in the Book of Life.

Revelation 17:9–14 Revealed

Verse 9 begins by informing us that the harlot sits on seven heads which are seven mountains. As we have become familiar with certain symbols, we know that heads, mountains, and kings are an example of world leaders.

- However, verse 9 switches from using the word "mountains" to using "kings" in verse 10. While the seven mountains serve under the Antichrist, the word "mountain" is used to describe the kings in the highest authority. Therefore, the seven kings mentioned in verse 10 don't serve under the Antichrist because they are not of the highest authority.
- Then verse 10 gives us a period in which these seven lesser kings reign—five have already fallen during John's day, one is in power in his day, and one is yet to reign in the future. We're told that this coming king is to remain a little while, pointing to the three and half years in the second half of tribulation.
- Then we're introduced to the beast in verse 11 who seems to occupy two positions since we're told that he is one of the seven and also an eighth. This is why he's described as the one who was and is not, referring to his death and

resurrection. So he occupies the place of the seventh until he dies, and when he resurrects, he holds the position of the eighth king.

- To gain a clearer understanding of the seven heads spoken of in verse 1, we'll need to skip back to Revelation 13:2, which speaks of the beast. The beast being described there is the same beast being described in Revelation 17, which also bears aspects of Daniel's vision of a leopard with the feet of a bear and the mouth of a lion. The seven kings include King Nebuchadnezzar of Babylon, King Cyrus and King Alexander of Persia, the Ptolemaic Kingdom, and the Seleucid Empire. General Titus would be the sixth king who would then become the emperor of Rome. As we mentioned earlier, the seventh and eighth would be the beast who was and is not.
- We then move on to verse 12 which speaks of the 10 horns which are 10 kings who don't receive their own kingdom but gain authority to rule with the beast for one hour, meaning a very short period. Verse 13 confirms their joint purpose to give their power and authority to the Antichrist, since they are serving his kingdom. They don't last very long, however, as their kingdoms will be destroyed with the coming of Christ.

Revelation 17:15–18 Revealed

Though the relationship between the mother of harlots and the Antichrist is stronger now more than ever, verse 15–16 shows us that there is no honor among thieves. After confirming that the waters she sits on are nations, we find that the 10 horns, or the world leaders, and the Antichrist betray her and begin to hate her.

The Antichrist's aim is to be worshiped and praised, so his agenda is to put himself in the position to receive such praise and adoration. As a result, all other forms of worship and religious practice must be abolished. And to accomplish this, all temples, churches, and mosques giving worship to other deities must be destroyed. These physical structures will be burned with fire, as we are told in verse 16, which strips away the wealth of the harlot, making her "desolate and naked."

Revelation 17:17 then lets us know that God is the one who has influenced the hearts of these kings to work in unison by giving their kingdoms to the beast and betraying the mother of Harlots. So in reality, they are fulfilling God's will even though they think they're acting independently of Him. With spiritual Babylon now out of the way, the only false religion left on earth is the worship of Satan through the Antichrist and the false prophet. And this will all be accomplished now that the seventh bowl has been poured out.

Throughout the Bible, God is known to use our enemies against each other to further His own agenda. So by allowing the kings of the earth and the Antichrist to destroy spiritual Babylon and all false religions, that's one less task of eradicating all false religions on earth that the Lord has to do. His only aim now would be to destroy the Antichrist, the false prophet, and the armies of the kings serving under him.

And with that, let's proceed to the 18th chapter of Revelation where Babylon the Great is being brought down in dramatic fashion.

End-of-Chapter Quiz

1. Why is Babylon symbolized as the mother of harlots?
2. How is spiritual Babylon instrumental in the Antichrist's rise to power?
3. What is inside the cup the harlot is drunk off of?
4. What will eventually happen to Babylon the mother of harlots?
5. Which bowl of judgment is causing this to happen?

Answers

1. Babylon is called the mother of harlots because she is responsible for many false religions and is the chief of them all. She has also committed fornication with the nations by sharing the wine of her demonic doctrine with those nations.
2. After the Antichrist receives a deadly wound and is healed or rather resurrected and indwelled with Satan, he allows Babylon the harlot to ride him so that he can be promoted as the only god on earth to be worshiped, forming a one world religion.
3. The harlot's cup is filled with the blood of the saint throughout history and during the tribulation.
4. The 10 horns who are the kings of the earth betray the harlot and give their authority to the beast.
5. All these things are happening as a result of the seventh bowl judgment.

18

REVELATION 18—THE FALL OF BABYLON

REVELATION 18:1–24

Lament Over Fallen Babylon
After this I saw another angel coming down from heaven. He had great authority, and the earth was illuminated by his splendor. With a mighty voice he shouted: "'Fallen! Fallen is Babylon the Great!' She has become a dwelling for demons and a haunt for every impure spirit, a haunt for every unclean bird, a haunt for every unclean and detestable animal. For all the nations have drunk the maddening wine of her adulteries. The kings of the earth committed adultery with her, and the merchants of the earth grew rich from her excessive luxuries."

Warning to Escape Babylon's Judgment
Then I heard another voice from heaven say: "'Come out of

her, my people,' so that you will not share in her sins, so that you will not receive any of her plagues; for her sins are piled up to heaven, and God has remembered her crimes. Give back to her as she has given; pay her back double for what she has done. Pour her a double portion from her own cup. Give her as much torment and grief as the glory and luxury she gave herself. In her heart she boasts, 'I sit enthroned as queen. I am not a widow; I will never mourn.' Therefore in one day her plagues will overtake her: death, mourning and famine. She will be consumed by fire, for mighty is the Lord God who judges her.

Threefold Woe Over Babylon's Fall

"When the kings of the earth who committed adultery with her and shared her luxury see the smoke of her burning, they will weep and mourn over her. Terrified at her torment, they will stand far off and cry: "'Woe! Woe to you, great city, you mighty city of Babylon! In one hour your doom has come!' "The merchants of the earth will weep and mourn over her because no one buys their cargoes anymore—cargoes of gold, silver, precious stones and pearls; fine linen, purple, silk and scarlet cloth; every sort of citron wood, and articles of every kind made of ivory, costly wood, bronze, iron and marble; cargoes of cinnamon and spice, of incense, myrrh and frankincense, of wine and olive oil, of fine flour and wheat; cattle and sheep; horses and carriages; and human beings sold as slaves. "They will say, 'The fruit you longed for is gone from you. All your luxury and splendor have vanished, never to be recovered.' The merchants who sold these things and gained their wealth from her will stand far off, terrified at her torment. They will weep and mourn and cry out: "'Woe! Woe to you, great city, dressed in fine linen, purple and scarlet, and glittering with gold, precious stones and pearls! In one hour such great wealth has been brought to ruin!' "Every sea captain, and all who travel by ship, the sailors, and all who earn their living from the sea, will stand far off. When they see the smoke of her burning, they will exclaim, 'Was there ever a city like this great city?' They will throw dust on their heads, and with weeping and mourning cry out: "'Woe! Woe to you, great city, where all who had ships on the sea became rich through her wealth! In one hour she has been brought to ruin!' "Rejoice over her, you heavens! Rejoice, you people of God! Rejoice, apostles and prophets! For God has judged her with the judgment she imposed on you."

The Finality of Babylon's Doom

Then a mighty angel picked up a boulder the size of a large millstone and threw it into the sea, and said: "With such violence the great city of Babylon will be thrown down, never to be found again. The music of harpists and musicians, pipers and trumpeters, will never be heard in you again. No worker of any trade will ever be found in you again. The sound of a millstone will never be heard in you again. The light of a lamp will never shine in you again. The voice of bridegroom and bride will never be heard in you again. Your merchants were the world's important people. By your magic spell all the nations were led astray. In her was found the blood of prophets and of God's holy people, of all who have been slaughtered on the earth."

Revelation 18:1–3 Revealed

Picking up from the last chapter, we ended by revealing the strategic plan of God to allow Babylon the Great, the mother of harlots aka spiritual Babylon, to be made utterly desolate by the seven world rulers who have given their allegiance to the Antichrist. With these kings cleansing the earth of false religions, Christ only has to concern Himself with coming back to destroy Satan, the Antichrist, and the false prophet personally.

Let's now dissect the epic fall of Babylon and the angelic assistance that spearheads this spiritually decadent system.

Revelation 18:1 begins with John seeing another glorious angel with authority coming down from heaven. The verse begins by saying, "After these things," which implies that the events of Chapter 18 are the result of events that happened in earlier chapters. If you were following the chapter-by-chapter sequence of judgments, you'll remember that the seventh bowl was already poured out toward the end of Chapter 16. However, as the effects of the seventh bowl judgment began to cause the fall of Babylon, there was an interruption in the description of those judgments as John was whisked away to get a brief history lesson on the harlot and to witness her being judged.

Now in Chapter 18, John returns to the literal, dramatic description of the great city being judged and the effects caused by the seventh bowl. So in continuation of verse 1, the angel with authority which came down from heaven cries with a loud voice that Babylon has fallen, repeating it twice for emphasis. He goes on to describe the spiritual atmosphere of Babylon, having become a dwelling place of demons and unclean spirits that will be imprisoned there. There is also mention of it being a place of unclean birds, or scavenger birds, implying that only dead things will remain in Babylon.

God had appointed the fall of Babylon long ago and had prophesied it through his prophets, namely, Isaiah, Jeremiah, and Ezekiel. For example:

- Isaiah 13:19–22 speaks in detail about how Babylon, once the most glorious and beautiful of kingdoms, will end up like when God destroyed Sodom and Gomorrah. It will never again be inhabited and will be a dwelling place for desert creatures like owls and ostriches (scavenger birds), as well as hyenas and jackals (scavenger dogs) and goats.
- A similar description is given in Jeremiah 51:35–37 where the Lord speaks of exacting vengeance upon Babylon on behalf of the inhabitants of Zion by making her fountain dry (like a desert). As a result, it will be the place of desert animals like jackals and without inhabitants, as it says in Jeremiah 51:37.
- But as expected, these animals are symbolic in meaning, and we can connect that truth to Chapter 18. Although the animals mentioned in Isaiah and Jeremiah are not listed in Revelation 18, what is mentioned is the demons and unclean spirits that will be dwelling in Babylon. As some may know, goats and unclean birds like crows, vultures, and owls are associated with sorcery and witchcraft. So the Lord is saying that Babylon will be a place filled with witchcraft and occultism while God's spirit will be removed.

As we proceed to verse 3, we are given three reasons for the destruction of Babylon:

1. The nations have become drunk with the wine of her immorality and adulteries. Babylon's influence has corrupted the nations of the world of that time, specifically the blasphemous worship of the beast.
2. Chapter 17:13 explained how the kings of the earth gave their authority to the beast that was carrying the harlot at the time. That authority included the political and military power that was handed over to Babylon in submission to the Antichrist.
3. The merchants of the world have shared in profiting from the wealth of the Antichrist's economic system in Babylon. With a new financial system in place known as the mark of the beast, the Antichrist could not wield an oppressive financial control over the nations, becoming wealthy as a result. By default, the nations in agreement with this new financial system also became wealthy.

Revelation 18:4–8 Revealed

Heading into verse 4, the short reign of glory and wealth would be coming to an end for Babylon and the nations in partnership with her and the Antichrist.

A loud voice from the heavenly realm is heard, warning God's people to come out and be separate from Babylon so as to not receive the plagues poured out by the seventh bowl by participating in her sins. The plagues have come upon the whole world except for the Jews, believers in Christ, and Jerusalem. Therefore, the clarion call is being made for any of God's people living in Babylon to flee before judgment strikes. Failure to do so will cause them to partake in the judgment.

- An example of the Lord sparing His people from the judgment of the wicked can be seen throughout the Bible. 2 Peter 2:9–10 tells us plainly: Then the Lord knows how to rescue the godly from trials and to hold the unrighteous for punishment on the day of judgment. This is especially true of those who follow the corrupt desire of the flesh and despise authority.

Babylon's destruction is coming not only because she has been married to the Antichrist but also for her history of opposing Israel, oppressing the true saints of God, and corrupting the world with spiritual harlotry.

Her judgment will therefore be twofold—one at the hands of men directed at the citizens of Babylon. The second will be accomplished supernaturally by the bowl judgments of God and directed against the structure of Babylon.

The book of Jeremiah 50:41–42 gives us a clue of where these men of war will be coming from to desecrate Babylon. Verse 1 says that a great nation from the north with many kings will be roused against her. They are described as cruel and without mercy and are arrayed like men for battle against the city.

Jeremiah 51:27–28 gives us even more detail of the geographic location of these nations, and the kingdoms on Ararat (Turkey), Minni

(Armenia), Ashkenaz (southern Russia), and the Medes are mentioned which are all kingdoms north of Babylon (Mesopotamia). Today, the nations found north of Babylon are Iran (Persia), Turkey, Armenia, and Russia. And non-coincidentally, as of late, some of these nations have been the topic of discussion in the realm of possible world war.

In Revelation 18:6, the voice from heaven is actually instructing those nations to pay back Babylon double for the deeds she has done because her sins have accumulated and God has remembered her iniquities.

We also get the sense in Revelation 18:7 that Babylon feels untouchable and has glorified herself, saying to herself, "I sit enthroned as queen. I am not a widow; I will never mourn." But little does she know that the Lord has orchestrated armies of men to turn against the Antichrist and attack his headquarters—Babylon. Following the attack on Babylon from the kings of the earth, the Lord will conclude the destruction of Babylon with His supernatural judgment, which is described in the rest of Chapter 18.

Revelation 18:9–20 Revealed

Verse 9 commences with a picture of the kings of the earth who enjoyed the spoils of immorality with Babylon lamenting over her for the rising smoke of her destruction. So we know, without a doubt, that the city is burning and the destruction has affected all three classes of society.

- The kings of the earth, who are probably the same world leaders who gave their allegiance to the Antichrist, are now

standing at a distance mourning for the great city of Babylon.
- Even the merchants in verse 11 are weeping over the wealth that will be lost because of the loss of trade with her.
- Verses 15–17 also sees the working class merchants, both on land and on sea, standing afar off in dismay because of the great wealth that has been laid waste.
- It's clear that despite her spiritual corruption, many nations profited from the wealth of Babylon.

The level of destruction upon Babylon causes everyone, including the kings who turned against her, to mourn from a distance. This tells us that the magnitude of this judgment was not caused by weapons of war but the supernatural judgment of God.

That's the reason we are told three times that the destruction of the city came in one hour. If this level of swift destruction was caused by invading armies, their leaders would not be lamenting at a safe distance, away from the desecration. Their actions show that they too have experienced God's wrath through the bowl judgment.

Back in Revelation 16:19, we find that the judgment even causes the great city to split into three parts. That's enough to make the fiercest military leader take cover at a safe distance.

Then Revelation 18:20 tells the saints, prophets, and apostles to rejoice over Babylon while the world mourns, because He has pronounced judgment on her for their sakes.

Revelation 18:21–24 Revealed

To give a visual comparison of what the Lord does to Babylon, John sees a strong angel in Revelation 18:21 cast a stone that looks like a millstone into the sea. He then says that in such a violent manner will Babylon be thrown down and will no longer be found. When a stone is thrown into the water, it sinks to the bottom and is seen no more, and this is what the Lord intends for Babylon.

He promises that no musician, harpist, or craftsman will be found in Babylon, nor will the light of a lamp shine there any longer. In short, she will be utterly laid waste.

And in verse 24, we are reminded that the reason for this terrible judgment is because she has shed the blood of prophets and saints throughout history.

As Chapter 18 comes to a close, we've gotten a close-up of the complete destruction of Babylon by the hands of the Antichrist's allies. The city is intended to be an utter wasteland because of the sorcery and abomination the Harlot has spread through the nations. And as we enter Chapter 19, we'll be informed of heaven's preparation for Christ's return and, with that, the Antichrist's desperate attempt to stop it.

End-of-Chapter Quiz

1. What is meant in verse 2 that Babylon has become a dwelling place of unclean spirits and unclean birds?
2. Why is Babylon compared to Sodom and Gomorrah is Isaiah 13:19?

3. What are two reasons why Babylon is being destroyed?
4. Why are God's people asked to flee Babylon before judgment knocks on her door?
5. Why are the kings and merchants of the earth observing Babylon burn from a distance?

Answers

1. What is being communicated is that the spiritual atmosphere of Babylon is one of death, sorcery, and witchcraft. A scavenger is known as an unclean bird because it feeds on dead things, meaning that Babylon is full of death.
2. Sodom and Gomorrah were completely destroyed by God in the Old Testament, and no one has inhabited that region to this day, and the same fate will befall Babylon.
3. Babylon is being destroyed for corrupting the nations of the world with her adulteries and idolatry and for encouraging the people of earth to worship the Antichrist.
4. Although they are protected from the plagues, the Jews and believing Gentiles are told to flee because staying in Babylon will cause them to partake in her judgment.
5. The kings and merchants are standing at a distance because of the severity of the judgment God poured out on Babylon.

19

REVELATION 19—THE RETURN OF CHRIST

REVELATION 19:1–21

Threefold Hallelujah Over Babylon's Fall

After this I heard what sounded like the roar of a great multitude in heaven shouting: "Hallelujah! Salvation and glory and power belong to our God, for true and just are his judgments. He has condemned the great prostitute who corrupted the earth by her adulteries. He has avenged on her the blood of his servants." And again they shouted: "Hallelujah! The smoke from her goes up for ever and ever." The twenty-four elders and the four living creatures fell down and worshiped God, who was seated on the throne. And they cried: "Amen, Hallelujah!" Then a voice came from the throne, saying: "Praise our God, all you his servants, you who fear him, both great and small!" Then I heard what sounded like a great multitude, like the roar of rushing waters and like loud peals of thunder, shouting: "Hallelujah! For our Lord God Almighty reigns. Let us rejoice and be glad and give him glory! For the wedding of the Lamb has come, and his bride has made herself ready. Fine linen, bright and clean, was given her to wear." (Fine linen stands for the righteous acts of God's holy people.) Then the angel said to me, "Write this: Blessed are those who are invited to the wedding supper of the Lamb!" And he added, "These are the true words of God." At this I fell at his feet to worship him. But he said to me, "Don't do that! I am a fellow servant with you and with your brothers and sisters who hold to the testimony of Jesus. Worship God! For it is the Spirit of prophecy who bears testimony to Jesus."

The Heavenly Warrior Defeats the Beast

I saw heaven standing open and there before me was a white horse, whose rider is called Faithful and True. With justice he judges and wages war. His eyes are like blazing fire, and on his head are many crowns. He has a name written on him that no one knows but he himself. He is dressed in a robe dipped in blood, and his name is the Word of God. The armies of heaven were following him, riding on white horses and dressed in fine linen, white and clean. Coming out of his mouth is a sharp sword with which to strike down the nations. "He will rule them with an iron scepter." He treads the winepress of the fury of the wrath of God Almighty. On his robe and on his thigh he has this name written: KING OF KINGS AND LORD OF LORDS. And I saw an angel standing in the sun, who cried in a loud voice to all the birds

> flying in midair, "Come, gather together for the great supper of God, so that you may eat the flesh of kings, generals, and the mighty, of horses and their riders, and the flesh of all people, free and slave, great and small." Then I saw the beast and the kings of the earth and their armies gathered together to wage war against the rider on the horse and his army. But the beast was captured, and with it the false prophet who had performed the signs on its behalf. With these signs he had deluded those who had received the mark of the beast and worshiped its image. The two of them were thrown alive into the fiery lake of burning sulfur. The rest were killed with the sword coming out of the mouth of the rider on the horse, and all the birds gorged themselves on their flesh.

Revelation 19:1–5 Revealed

Just as in Chapter 18, John begins Revelation 19:1 with "after these things," which in Greek is *meta houte houtos* and implies a cause-and-effect sequence from the previous chapter. As we mentioned, Chapter 19 will be focusing on the return of Christ to earth. And of course, certain developments had to take place first, mainly the pouring out of the seventh bowl judgment.

The details of the effects of the seventh bowl judgment are found between Chapters 16 and 18, and a few of the events that cleared the way for the Lord's Second Coming were the removal of the Antichrist's military forces out of Babylon and into northern Israel in preparation to wage war against the Jews to hopefully stop Christ's return.

Instead, this allowed for the Antichrist capital, Babylon, to be exposed which spawned an attack by a few of his treacherous allies. The destruction of Babylon has cleared the way for Christ to return since one of the key opponents on the chess mat has been removed. And so preparation for His return begins with the marriage supper of the Lamb. We see in verse 1 that there is great jubilation in heaven, with a great multitude singing hallelujah! Heaven is rejoicing greatly over the fall of Babylon who has now been judged by God for shedding the blood of the bond servants of Christ.

They are evermore certain that all power and glory belong to God for avenging those who were martyred on earth and for judging all things immoral and ungodly on earth. Then, for a second time in verse 3, they give a shout of praise as they rejoice over the destruction of Babylon.

Even the four living creatures and the 24 elders worship the Lord who sits on the throne, shouting, "Amen. Hallelujah!" Worship is one of the dominant means of communication in heaven because it comes from a pure place in a child of God who is grateful for God's goodness, mercy, wisdom, power, and grace.

For believers alive today, worship should not only be an inward emotion that causes us to break out in song. Worship should encompass a lifestyle purposed by the outward expression of devotion to our Savior.

Revelation 19:6–10 Revealed

The multitude continues their joint expression of praise to the Father from Revelation 19:6–8.

They jubilate and give glory to God for the marriage supper of the Lamb that is almost underway. The bride, which is the church, has made herself ready for the Lamb.

From this, the term "bride of Christ" has been coined as a New Testament reference to born-again, Spirit-filled church saints who keep faith in Jesus Christ.

We are given a clear reference of the relationship that Christ seeks to cultivate with the church in the Book of Ephesians 5:25–27, which reads:

> Husbands, love your wives, just as Christ loved the church and gave himself up for her to make her holy, cleansing her by the washing with water through the word, and to present her to himself as a radiant church, without stain or wrinkle or any other blemish, but holy and blameless.

The Lord refers to the church as the bride and Himself as the groom as a metaphor for the way He desires to be one with His people. That's the reason why only those with the Holy Spirit dwelling in them are considered the bride of Christ. Because His spirit dwells in us, we are one with Him, similar to how a man and woman become one flesh in an earthly marriage.

Verse 8 can also be referenced by Ephesians 5:27 which shows us that the church has made herself ready, having no spot or wrinkle on her garment. She has been made holy and blameless in fine linen, bright and clean, which represents our works as believers.

And like most weddings, there will be guests invited to witness the marriage ceremony. John is told in verse 9, "Blessed are those who are invited to the wedding supper of the Lamb!" So the next logical question would be, who are the guests that are invited to the greatest wedding ceremony in history?

Since the bride can't be invited to attend her own wedding, the Old Testament and tribulation saints will most likely be those in attendance. Since these saints will be awaiting resurrection, which hasn't happened as yet, they will be in spirit form.

Overwhelmed by the jubilation and magnificence of heaven, John bows down to worship his escort angel but is quickly urged to stop. He understands that he is just a messenger who holds the testimony of Jesus Christ, just like John does.

The angel knows that for John to worship him would be idolatry. Instead, he tells John to worship God because the testimony of Jesus is the spirit of prophecy. Jesus is the source, and he is merely the vessel.

Revelation 19:11–16 Revealed

As we launch into Revelation 19, the main focus is a topic every believer anticipates, and that's the return of Christ. However, this joyous and historic event is met by the demonic resistance of the Antichrist and his remaining military subjects on earth. This resistance sparks one of the most renowned and, frankly, one of the most asinine wars man has fought in history—The war of Armageddon. The war concludes the seven-year tribulation and marks the end of the Antichrist's rule on earth.

Let's quickly recap the sequence of events that lead up to the Lord's return:

- The sixth bowl judgment sparks the first stage of the war of Armageddon by drying up the Euphrates River so that the Antichrist and his military muscle could be baited to leave Babylon and set up camp in the Jezreel Valley in an attempt to invade Jerusalem.
- As he settles in the Jezreel Valley and prepares to martyr the remaining Jews in Jerusalem and Petra, the Lord uses this opportunity to deliver the seventh bowl judgment on Babylon, reducing it to an ash heap. This leaves the Antichrist with no choice but to march forward with attacking Jerusalem.
- The Antichrist moves to a point between the great sea and the holy mountain and surrounds the city of Jerusalem from the point. The weapons of warfare have been reduced to a rudimentary level due to the tribulation. Believe it or not, the Antichrist uses horses, swords, and other medieval war weapons. As a result, the Jews in Jerusalem are protected by the walls of the city.
- Despite the Antichrist's attempts, the Lord supernaturally defends the Jews from his attacks, which will cause them to repent and put their faith in Christ.
- By now, the Antichrist is desperate to destroy the remnant of Israel in Petra, which is where the Lord prepared to keep them safe during the last three and a half years of tribulation. He does this using the remaining military forces in Babylon to overtake the Jewish inhabitants there.

Now that we have a basic picture of the Antichrist's positioning on earth prior to Christ's return, let's begin with Revelation 19:11

which speaks of Christ's return to earth a second time to save His people.

- John gives us a vantage point from earth where he sees heaven itself open up and the Lord appears leading His heavenly army in preparation for war. His eyes are like a flame of fire and on His head are many crowns. His overall visage is in the same glorified form as He appeared in Chapter 1.
- He also has a name written on Him which no one knows but Himself. Today, we call Him Yeshua or Jesus, but He will bear a different name upon His return.

John also witnesses Christ riding on a white horse, which the Bible uses as a symbol of royalty and rulership. From the following description, we quickly get the impression that He means business. The role of the sacrificial Lamb has been fulfilled, and the lion of Judah has come to rule and reign:

- This seems like a familiar scene, as John also saw the counterfeit Christ, the Antichrist, also riding on a white horse in Revelation 6 at the opening of the first seal.
- However, He is wearing a robe dipped in blood, signifying the battle that will be waged while showing that the true Messiah has arrived, and His name is the Word of God.

John tells us in verse 15 that a sharp sword proceeds from His mouth, with which He will strike down the nations that oppose Him and rule with a rod of iron.

- The sharp sword in His mouth we know to be the Word of God, which is referenced in Ephesians 6:17 as the sword of the Spirit.
- He is also coming to tread the winepress of God Almighty. It's clear that He is coming to wage war.
- We're told in Revelation 16:14 that the heavenly armies arrayed behind Him are clothed in fine, white linen and are also riding on white horses.
- The believers occupy the armies following Christ and are accompanying Him to rule and reign on earth. However, although we are called an army, Jesus will need none of our help to defeat the Antichrist and his armies.
- After he single-handedly defeats the Antichrist and saves Israel, the seven-year tribulation will be concluded. Such a great accomplishment then begins the transition of the earth's rulership into the hands of Jesus as His kingdom will now be set up following His return.

Revelation 19:17–21 Revealed

As John is relaying His vision, we are being given a heavenly perspective of Christ's return as well as the activities of the Antichrist and his armies on earth. However, the Old Testament prophets gave us an earthly account of these events.

- Continuing with verse 17, the scriptures paint a picture of the carnage left in the aftermath of the war of Armageddon. The number of dead bodies is so great that an angel standing in the sun is calling to all the birds that fly in midheaven to assemble for a feast. Although this

angel uses the term midheaven, it's not the same as when previously mentioned, where it was pointing to outer space.
- The angel is calling these birds to eat the flesh of dead carcasses of kings, commanders, horses, and men of all classes. We can imagine these birds to be vultures, which are known to scavenge on dead carcasses. Consider these birds the cleanup crew for the great slaughter left in the wake of the war.

So without barely breaking a sweat, Jesus laid waste the armies of the Antichrist and saved the Jews who were kept preserved in Petra for the latter part of the seven-year tribulation.

Now, it came time to seize the Antichrist and the false prophet and cast them headlong into the lake of fire. Though they operated through human vehicles, the Antichrist was a conduit for Satan and the false prophet a willing vessel for a powerful demon. Only an evil presence could have conspired to lead mankind to defy the Almighty to fulfill a lustful desire to be worshiped like God.

Just as anyone else who dies, the spirit leaves the body. And the same applies to the Antichrist and the false prophet. Isaiah 14:1–21 tells us some of the account of Satan's arrival in hell. He is despised even by the captains and kings who fought for him. And despite his pride and defiance to God, he is reminded of how small and insignificant he truly is and how he too must share in their torment.

He and the false prophet enter hell alive, meaning all their senses are intact. They are immediately given a new, eternal body, just as believers will receive a new, glorified body after leaving their earthly bodies. However, the Antichrist (Satan) will only be bound for a short time in hell. He will be released again after the 1,000-year reign of Christ, but we'll dissect this more in the coming chapter.

End-of-Chapter Quiz

1. What events had to take place before Christ's Second Coming?
2. Who makes up the armies of Christ accompanying Him on His return?
3. Why is the church referred to as the bride of Christ?
4. Why does Jesus wear a robe dipped in blood upon His return?
5. What happens after the Antichrist (Satan) and the false prophet are cast into hell?

Answers

1. Before Christ returns, the Antichrist's military forces need to be drawn to the valley of Jezreel so they can attack Israel, leaving Babylon vulnerable for destruction.
2. The angels of God and the saints (you and I hopefully) will be riding on white horses with Jesus as our King and commander.
3. The church is called the bride of Christ because Jesus wants to be the groom who marries His people so that we become one, in the same way that a man and woman become one when they are married.

4. The robe dipped in blood is meant to signify the blood that will be shed after waging war against the Antichrist and his armies.
5. They are given a new spiritual body where they will live out their eternal existence in torment and fire.

20

REVELATION 20—SATAN BOUND

REVELATION 20:1–15

The Thousand Years

And I saw an angel coming down out of heaven, having the key to the Abyss and holding in his hand a great chain. He seized the dragon, that ancient serpent, who is the devil, or Satan, and bound him for a thousand years. He threw him into the Abyss, and locked and sealed it over him, to keep him from deceiving the nations anymore until the thousand years were ended. After that, he must be set free for a short time. I saw thrones on which were seated those who had been given authority to judge. And I saw the souls of those who had been beheaded because of their testimony about Jesus and because of the word of God. They had not worshiped the beast or its image and had not received its mark on their foreheads or their hands. They came to life and reigned with Christ a thousand years. (The rest of the dead did not come to life until the thousand years were ended.) This is the first resurrection. Blessed and holy are those who share in the first resurrection. The second death has no power over them, but they will be priests of God and of Christ and will reign with him for a thousand years.

The Judgment of Satan
When the thousand years are over, Satan will be released from his prison and will go out to deceive the nations in the four corners of the earth—Gog and Magog—and to gather them for battle. In number they are like the sand on the seashore. They marched across the breadth of the earth and surrounded the camp of God's people, the city he loves. But fire came down from heaven and devoured them. And the devil, who deceived them, was thrown into the lake of burning sulfur, where the beast and the false prophet had been thrown. They will be tormented day and night for ever and ever.

The Judgment of the Dead
Then I saw a great white throne and him who was seated on it. The earth and the heavens fled from his presence, and there was no place for them. And I saw the dead, great and small, standing before the throne, and books were opened. Another book was opened, which is the book of life. The dead were judged according to what they had done as recorded in the books. The sea gave up the dead that were in it, and death and Hades gave up the dead that were in them, and each person was judged according to what they had

> done. Then death and Hades were thrown into the lake of fire. The lake of fire is the second death. Anyone whose name was not found written in the book of life was thrown into the lake of fire.

Revelation 20:1–3 Revealed

As you can expect, the feeling of euphoria and festivity is in the air now that the accuser of the brethren, Satan, has been defeated and cast into the lake of fire along with the false prophet. The Lord has recently won the war of Armageddon, and now, Satan's old-world order must also be done away with. The unbelievers (those who have received the mark of the beast and worshiped the image of the Antichrist) were also killed by the sword of Christ's mouth and joined their god in the lake of fire, as Revelation 19:21 tells us.

Now that the 1,290 days, or three and a half years, spoken of by Daniel have come to an end, the tribulation is officially finished. However, Daniel 12:11 tells us to count 1,290 days from the mid-tribulation until the abomination of desolation has ended.

When the Antichrist stopped the daily sacrifice at the temple in Jerusalem, he and the false prophet set up his image to be worshiped. So beginning from His return, Jesus has 30 days to remove the image, which is 1,290 days after mid-tribulation.

This is just another part of the cleanup process that must ensue so that Christ's kingdom can be established. The cleanup campaign already began when the angel called the birds to feast on the cadavers of the Antichrist's army, and more must be done to bring in a new heaven and a new earth.

Isaiah 65:17–19 also confirms the 30-day cleanup campaign to cleanse the earth of all uncleanness following the postwar disaster:

> See, I will create new heavens and a new earth. The former things will not be remembered, nor will they come to mind. But be glad and rejoice forever in what I will create, for I will create Jerusalem to be a delight and its people a joy. I will rejoice over Jerusalem and take delight in my people; the sound of weeping and of crying will be heard in it no more.

That being said, let's head over to Revelation 20:1 to see how the cleansing process is going.

- In verse 1, John beholds an angel coming down from heaven with the key to the abyss and a great chain in his hand. It's important to note that although Christ and His joint army of angels and saints arrive on earth, there is still angelic activity taking place from the throne room in heaven, which means the Father is still there.
- As Christ has come to set up His kingdom on earth for the 1,000-year reign, the Father will remain in the heavenly realm because sin will still be present on the earth. Therefore, Christ will still be the medium for anyone to see the Father until He comes to earth to reunite with His Son, which will be covered in Chapter 21.

Going back to the angel in verse 1, he is coming with the key to the abyss and the chain so that Satan can be bound for 1,000 years, which is the same amount of time for the 1,000-year reign of peace with Christ on earth. The abyss has been mentioned numerous times in the Book of Revelation and has been found to be a place where demons and fallen angels are imprisoned. This is confirmed in Chapter 9 verse 1, where Satan himself once held the key to the bottomless pit, but now, he is placed in confinement.

For a short while after the 1,000-year reign of peace, Satan will be loosed to remove peace from the earth, as stated in Revelation 20:3. And after that, Satan and all the demons and fallen angels will be released from the abyss to receive their final verdict in the lake of fire. Hell, or Sheol, will also be emptied of the human souls housed therein to receive final judgment before being cast into the lake of fire.

Revelation 20:4 Revealed

Now that Satan has been bound, John's vision switches to seeing thrones being set up for the souls who had been beheaded for their testimony of Jesus Christ, which were mentioned in Revelation 6. These are the tribulation saints who were among the first to be martyred for their faith before the Antichrist assumed full political power.

Also present were the souls of those who did not worship the image of the beast or receive his mark in their hand or forehead. John also mentioned later in the verse that the souls of those saints "came to life." But we know that souls never die to begin with, so what John is describing is the resurrection, where their souls will receive a new, glorified body.

After they receive their thrones and glorified bodies, they are now ready to reign during the 1,000-year reign with Christ.

Revelation 20:5–7 Revealed

With the resurrection of the dead in Christ complete, verse 5 lets us know that the rest of the dead did not come to life until after the 1,000 years were complete. The resurrection of the believers is called the first resurrection, and there is also a resurrection for unbelievers, but the phrasing of "first" and "second" refers to the times of judgment. Preceding the judgment of the believers is their resurrection, which is basically their entrance pass into the kingdom.

The second resurrection of the unbelievers will take place after the 1,000 years have ended. As we've mentioned, they will not be entering the kingdom but will be awaiting their final judgment before being cast into the lake of fire, which will mark the second judgment.

The Bible even says in Revelation 20:6 that those who have part in the first resurrection are blessed and holy and the second death will have no power over them. The second death here is referencing the second judgment of unbelievers, after which they will be tormented forever in the lake of fire. But on the contrary, those blessed to be a part of the first resurrection will reign as priests with God and Christ for 1,000 years.

Then we're informed in verse 7 that after the 1,000 years are completed, Satan will be released from his prison. Because the kingdom will also consist of natural-born men and women with flesh bodies, both Jew and Gentile, Satan will be allowed to tempt them once again for a short while before his final judgment to the fiery lake of torment. Rest assured that he will use his temporary release to incite another rebellion against God. One thing for sure is he is persistent!

Revelation 20:7–10 Revealed

As we've already stated, Revelation 20:7 confirms that Satan is now bound for 1,000 years, and once his time is served, he'll be released momentarily back into the new earth. But as we suspected, he will go forth to deceive the nations in all four corners of the earth, recruiting them for another war with Christ. This time, it's the war of Gog and Magog.

We know that Satan is everything Christ is not. So since Christ is the Way, the Truth, and the Life, Satan is the father of lies. So since he operates in deception, he will deceive Gog and Magog for a final war against the Lord.

But some may wonder, why doesn't Christ just give Satan the death penalty right away during the 1,000 years of peace? It's because for the last 6,000 years ever since the fall of Adam and Eve, the world has trusted in mankind. The Book of Jeremiah 17:5 even says, "Cursed is the one who trusts in man, who draws strength from mere flesh and whose heart turns away from the LORD." It's also worth pointing out that six in the Bible is the number for a sinful man.

The 1,000 years of peace will bring the age of the world to 7,000—seven being the number of perfection and completion. During the 1,000-year reign of Christ, the heavens and the earth will be made new under the rule of Jesus, proving that only through the Messiah comes true righteousness, justice, and peace.

Satan will be released after 1,000 years of perfection to deceive the nations so that creation too can come into completion and Christ can defeat the last enemy.

Now, returning to the identity of Gog and Magog, we are told in Revelation 20:8–9 that the number of this army will be as many as the sand of the seashore. They conspired together with Satan to surround the camp of the saints and Israel and were devoured by fire from heaven, similar to how the city of Babylon was destroyed.

- If you're a Bible student, you'll know that Gog and Magog were first mentioned in the Book of Ezekiel 38–39. We'll find in those scriptures that Gog is a title, like Pharaoh, and Magog is the nation he hails from, referring to Eastern Europe and present-day Turkey. Ezekiel 38:9–16 tells us further that Gog is enticed with an evil imagination from Satan to invade the land of Israel out of greed. God's people are dwelling safely in Israel in the kingdom and are abundant in land, cattle, and goods.
- Israel has always been the apple of God's eye, so they are blessed above any other land on earth, which makes Gog lustful and envious—both traits of Satan. And with the help of Satan, he recruits nations from the north to invade Israel. Those nations in the present day would include Russia, Turkey, Libya, Iran, and Ethiopia.
- However, as John relayed to us in Revelation 20:9, their entire multitude was destroyed by fire which the Lord sent down from heaven before they even had a chance to touch a strand of hair on any of the saints.

- Satan's plots to harm the people of God are foiled, and he loses again. This time, his judgment will be final, as we read in Revelation 20:10, that he was thrown into the lake of fire and brimstone, where he will accompany the beast and the false prophet in their never-ending cycle of torment.

Revelation 20:11–15 Revealed

Now that the end of the millennial reign of Christ had ended and Satan had been judged and disposed of in the lake of fire, it's time for the second resurrection, or the final judgment of the unbelievers from all of history, both great and small.

- Revelation 20:12 tells us that John saw the dead standing before the throne and they were judged according to their deeds by the Book of Life, which was opened before the Lord.
- We are also told that the dead from the sea resurrected and judged as well. But it's not talking about the actual sea where the fish died a few chapters ago. The Hebrew word being used for the sea is *tehom*, which translates to mean a pit, an abyss, or the sea. As we know, the abyss is the holding place for demons and fallen angels next to Hades in the center of the earth. So the great white throne judgment is all-encompassing, including both the souls of ungodly humans and the rebellious angels.
- Then we're told in verse 14 that death and Hades were themselves thrown into the lake of fire, which is the second death. So first, death and Hades gave up the souls that were being kept in its grasp to be judged, which was called the

first death. Since death and earth are passing away, Hades will no longer be needed to keep the souls of the ungodly. God is truly making all things new.

- The chapter ends with verse 15 letting us know anyone whose name was not found written in the Book of Life. We learned in Revelation 3:5 that God already has names written in the Book of Life. In the tribulation particularly, those who worshiped the Antichrist and took his mark were not found in the Book of Life, and the believers who did not overcome and hold true to their faith had their names removed.

End-of-Chapter Quiz

1. Why was Satan bound in the abyss for exactly 1,000 years?
2. Why hasn't the Father joined Christ on earth for the 1,000-year reign of peace?
3. What will happen to Satan after 1,000 years?
4. Who or what is Gog and Magog?

Answers

1. Satan was bound for 1,000 years in order to set up his Kingdom on earth for the millennial reign of Christ.
2. Until Christ has completely restored a new heaven and a new earth, sin will remain in the earth. And the Father cannot dwell among sin.
3. After his 1,000-year sentence, Satan and the fallen angels will be released from the abyss to tempt mankind for a

short time on the new earth before his final destination in the lake of fire.

4. Gog and Magog is known as the final battle between Christ and Satan. Gog is a title, similar to Pharaoh or Caesar, and Magog is the nation in present-day Turkey where Gog is from.

21

REVELATION 21—A NEW HEAVEN AND A NEW EARTH

REVELATION 21:1–27

A New Heaven and a New Earth

Then I saw "a new heaven and a new earth," for the first heaven and the first earth had passed away, and there was no longer any sea. I saw the Holy City, the new Jerusalem, coming down out of heaven from God, prepared as a bride beautifully dressed for her husband. And I heard a loud voice from the throne saying, "Look! God's dwelling place is now among the people, and he will dwell with them. They will be his people, and God himself will be with them and be their God. 'He will wipe every tear from their eyes. There will be no more death' or mourning or crying or pain, for the old order of things has passed away." He who was seated on the throne said, "I am making everything new!" Then he said, "Write this down, for these words are trustworthy and true." He said to me: "It is done. I am the Alpha and the Omega, the Beginning and the End. To the thirsty I will give water without cost from the spring of the water of life. Those who are victorious will inherit all this, and I will be their God and they will be my children. But the cowardly, the unbelieving, the vile, the murderers, the sexually immoral, those who practice magic arts, the idolaters and all liars—they will be consigned to the fiery lake of burning sulfur. This is the second death."

The New Jerusalem, the Bride of the Lamb
One of the seven angels who had the seven bowls full of the seven last plagues came and said to me, "Come, I will show you the bride, the wife of the Lamb." And he carried me away in the Spirit to a mountain great and high, and showed me the Holy City, Jerusalem, coming down out of heaven from God. It shone with the glory of God, and its brilliance was like that of a very precious jewel, like a jasper, clear as crystal. It had a great, high wall with twelve gates, and with twelve angels at the gates. On the gates were written the names of the twelve tribes of Israel. There were three gates on the east, three on the north, three on the south and three on the west. The wall of the city had twelve foundations, and on them were the names of the twelve apostles of the Lamb. The angel who talked with me had a measuring rod of gold to measure the city, its gates and its walls. The city was laid out like a square, as long as it was wide. He measured the city with the rod and found it to be 12,000 stadia in length, and as wide and high as it is long. The angel measured the wall using human measure-

> ment, and it was 144 cubits thick. The wall was made of jasper, and the city of pure gold, as pure as glass. The foundations of the city walls were decorated with every kind of precious stone. The first foundation was jasper, the second sapphire, the third agate, the fourth emerald, the fifth onyx, the sixth ruby, the seventh chrysolite, the eighth beryl, the ninth topaz, the tenth turquoise, the eleventh jacinth, and the twelfth amethyst. The twelve gates were twelve pearls, each gate made of a single pearl. The great street of the city was of gold, as pure as transparent glass. I did not see a temple in the city, because the Lord God Almighty and the Lamb are its temple. The city does not need the sun or the moon to shine on it, for the glory of God gives it light, and the Lamb is its lamp. The nations will walk by its light, and the kings of the earth will bring their splendor into it. On no day will its gates ever be shut, for there will be no night there. The glory and honor of the nations will be brought into it. Nothing impure will ever enter it, nor will anyone who does what is shameful or deceitful, but only those whose names are written in the Lamb's book of life.

Revelation 21:1–8 Revealed

With most of the systems of the old world gone, such as death and Hades, ungodliness and Satan, and other things that existed prior to Christ's return, heaven and earth are also on the list for a makeover. John is again relaying his vision to us, and this time, he sees a new heaven and a new earth. But unlike our present earth, there are no seas. Could this be the reason why some of the trumpet and bowl judgments targeted the sea and other bodies of water specifically? We'll find out more in the coming verses.

Next, the Lord has prepared the new Jerusalem for the new earth as a bride adorned for her husband. This will be the new holy city form where Christ will rule.

After that wonderful spectacle, John hears a loud voice in verse 3 stating that the tabernacle of God is now with men. This is a truly special time, since it will be the first time since Adam and Eve in the Garden of Eden that God will dwell among men. Verse 4 goes on to state that all of the consequences of sin and sin itself will no longer exist, such as death, tears, mourning, or pain. These all came as a consequence of Adam's sin after the fall of man and had kept the world in bondage up until the time of the restoration of heaven and earth.

Going forward in verse 6, Christ lets us know that He is the alpha and omega, the first and the last, and the beginning and the end. He also confirms His actions by declaring in Revelation 21:5 that He is making all things new.

Just as Jesus was the Word who was present during creation in the beginning, He is also the same at the end of time. And as the Creator of all things, He is making all things new on earth once again. He is truly the beginning and the ending of all things.

Further in the same verse, He reminds us that He is the giver of life and He will offer the spring of the water of life to anyone who is thirsty. In verse 7, He promises that those who overcome will inherit all things, since He is the Creator and all things exist because of Him. And just as He overcame when He first came to earth and sat at the right hand of the Father as the Son of God, He will also make the overcomer His Son.

Finally, in verse 8, He lists a number of sins that are prevalent in the lives of many unbelievers and assured that those who practice those sins will be cast into the lake of fire, which is now called the second death. Some of these since include murderers, immoral people, sorcerers, idolaters, and all liars. Unbelief is one of the sins named among the sins mentioned and they are all rooted in unbelief. And that is not the nature of believers. Everyone will still have free will, and so only those who chose to be unbelievers will exhibit these fruits.

Revelation 21:9–14 Revealed

John speaks with one of the angels who had the seven bowls of judgment and the seven last plagues, and the angel carried him away in the Spirit to show him the bride of the Lamb. In verse 10, he sees Jerusalem, the Holy City, coming down to earth from God in heaven. The city is called the bride of Christ, which is the name given to the body of Christ who will dwell with Christ in eternity.

Jesus built the Holy City for his saints, the bride of Christ, who will also be dwelling in the city. John gives some of the specifications of the building, stating that it is equal on all sides in length and width. The city is also surrounded by a high wall with three gates on each side, totaling 12 gates. There are also 12 foundation stones on the wall of the city bearing the names of the 12 apostles of Christ.

Normally, walls and gates are used as a defense to keep intruders out. But since all the enemies of the Lord have been judged, especially Satan who has been cast into the lake of fire, the gates are open continually, as we'll see later in verse 25.

Revelation 21:15–21 Revealed

From Revelation 21:15–21, John gives us much more detail about the measurements of the building and the materials used in its construction. He likens the architecture to that of a perfect square measuring 1,500 miles in length and width in each direction. What's more is that the city is designed as a cube and extends into the sky at the same measurement of 1,500 miles. With such an elevated height, the structure would be able to reach orbiting satellites in today's world.

The wall measures at 75 yards high, which is 144 cubits, while in "angelic measurement," it is 12,000 stadion. The amazing feature about the measurements is the fact that the city is built on 12s and multiples of 12, which is a commemoration to the 12 tribes of Israel and the 12 apostles. In the Bible, 12 represents God's perfect order through men.

And when it came to aesthetics and extravagance, this building was second to none with 12 foundation stones on each of the 12 gates, which include jasper, sapphire, chalcedony, emerald, sardonyx, sardius, chrysolite, topaz, chrysoprase, jacinth, and amethyst. Adding to the magnificence were the streets of gold which was so luminescent that it appeared like transparent glass. Isn't it ironic that the very precious metals that men strive today to acquire are one day going to be under our feet?

Revelation 21:22–27 Revealed

When God says He is making everything new, He is also including the manner of worship that once existed. Temples existed in the old world in order to separate man from God because sinful man could not dwell in the presence of a holy God. But as we read in Revelation 21:22, there will no longer be a need for a temple because the fullness of the Godhead is present, and the Father and the Son are the temple. As we mentioned previously, the Father is reunited with Christ and man again for the first time since Adam walked in the garden.

We also see in verse 23 that the Godhead is the source of light, so there will be no need for the sun and moon in the new earth. Even though in our present time the sun and the moon were sources of light that represented the glory of God and separated day from night, God Himself will be the glorious light in the new earth.

John adds in verse 24 that the nations will walk by this light, for the Lamb is the light and the kings of the earth will bring their glory into it. Since there will be no independent authorities, the kings of the earth will submit their authority back to God. And since there will be no opposing powers on earth, the gates will never be closed, as we see in Revelation 21:25.

There will also be no night at all, which would make sense since God is the life-giving source in the midst of everyone. This would also suggest that the new earth is not spherical, but flat, allowing the light of God to shine equally on the earth. This would also suggest that there will be no days and years to count, since there will no longer be any nights. Time would essentially be nonexistent.

And with that, we head into the final chapter of the Book of Revelation, Chapter 22. This chapter will be highlighting some of the awesome features to be expected in the Holy City.

End-of-Chapter Quiz

1. What is one thing the old earth had that the new earth won't have?
2. What are some of the sins and lifestyles that stem from unbelief?
3. What is the shape of the Holy City which came down from heaven?
4. Are there any unique features about the architecture of the Holy City?
5. What is one significant event that happens in Chapter 21 that hasn't happened since the Garden of Eden?

Answers

1. The new earth won't have any sea like the old earth.
2. Murder, immorality, sorcery, idolatry, and lying are all the fruit of unbelief.
3. The Holy City is shaped like a cube.
4. The Holy City is built like a perfect square measuring exactly 1,500 miles in length and width on all sides.
5. This would be the first time the Father dwelled with the Son on earth since the Garden of Eden in Genesis.

22

REVELATION 22—IN THE HOLY CITY

REVELATION 22:1–21

Eden Restored

Then the angel showed me the river of the water of life, as clear as crystal, flowing from the throne of God and of the Lamb down the middle of the great street of the city. On each side of the river stood the tree of life, bearing twelve crops of fruit, yielding its fruit every month. And the leaves of the tree are for the healing of the nations. No longer will there be any curse. The throne of God and of the Lamb will be in the city, and his servants will serve him. They will see his face, and his name will be on their foreheads. There will be no more night. They will not need the light of a lamp or the light of the sun, for the Lord God will give them light. And they will reign for ever and ever.

John and the Angel

The angel said to me, "These words are trustworthy and true. The Lord, the God who inspires the prophets, sent his angel to show his servants the things that must soon take place." "Look, I am coming soon! Blessed is the one who keeps the words of the prophecy written in this scroll." I, John, am the one who heard and saw these things. And when I had heard and seen them, I fell down to worship at the feet of the angel who had been showing them to me. But he said to me, "Don't do that! I am a fellow servant with you and with your fellow prophets and with all who keep the words of this scroll. Worship God!" Then he told me, "Do not seal up the words of the prophecy of this scroll, because the time is near. Let the one who does wrong continue to do wrong; let the vile person continue to be vile; let the one who does right continue to do right; and let the holy person continue to be holy."

Epilogue: Invitation and Warning

"Look, I am coming soon! My reward is with me, and I will give to each person according to what they have done. I am the Alpha and the Omega, the First and the Last, the Beginning and the End. "Blessed are those who wash their robes, that they may have the right to the tree of life and may go through the gates into the city. Outside are the dogs, those who practice magic arts, the sexually immoral, the murderers, the idolaters and everyone who loves and practices falsehood. "I, Jesus, have sent my angel to give you this testimony for the churches. I am the Root and the Offspring of David, and the bright Morning Star." The Spirit and the

> bride say, "Come!" And let the one who hears say, "Come!" Let the one who is thirsty come; and let the one who wishes take the free gift of the water of life. I warn everyone who hears the words of the prophecy of this scroll: If anyone adds anything to them, God will add to that person the plagues described in this scroll. And if anyone takes words away from this scroll of prophecy, God will take away from that person any share in the tree of life and in the Holy City, which are described in this scroll. He who testifies to these things says, "Yes, I am coming soon." Amen. Come, Lord Jesus. The grace of the Lord Jesus be with God's people. Amen.

Revelation 22:1–5 Revealed

Like any good husband, God has truly gone above and beyond for His bride. As we read, we'll find that Revelation 22:1 may be the reason why God removed the sea in the new earth. John is shown the river of the water of life, clear as crystal, flowing from the throne of God and into the city. It continues flowing into the middle of a wide street with the tree of life on either side of the river.

- Verse 2 then tells us that the tree bears a variety of fruit—12 to be exact—yielding a different fruit each month. But the fruit isn't the only desirable aspect of the tree of life, as the leaves also have healing powers that will be for the various nations of people in the new earth.

The last time we heard of the tree of life was in the book of Genesis 2:8–9 in the Garden of Eden. Genesis 2:9 says that it was planted by

God in the midst of the garden next to the tree of the knowledge of good and evil, the latter of which caused the fall of man.

- As we continue to verse 3, we're informed that there will no longer be any curses. This is important to note because shortly after Eve gave Adam of the fruit of the tree of the knowledge of good and evil, God curses the ground which leads to physical death, calamity, and eventual destruction of the earth. The curse has manifested itself for 6,000 years, and now that heaven and earth have been made new, it has been removed. There is no longer any condemnation as a result of sin and the world seems flawless. We know that the wages of sin is death. So without sin, there is no death.

Because we too have been made perfect, we will work in God's presence and see His face, something not even Moses was able to do while on earth because of man's fallen state. He also claims us as His own by marking His name on our foreheads, assuring us that we will never experience sin or face death ever again.

- We are again reminded in verse 5 that there will be no night, no need for light or the sun, because the Lord God will be our light for all eternity. There will be no fear of darkness or any shadow because He will be our continuous source of light.

We're told in 1 John 1:5 that "God is light; in him there is no darkness at all." So it begs the question, why did God create light and dark, day and night, in the first creation to begin with? It's because God, in His all-knowing nature, knew the first creation would be corrupted by sin in the garden and made provision by adding in certain features in anticipation of a fallen, sinful atmosphere. The design in the natural elements would also be manifested through the reality of sin and redemption and righteousness and wickedness.

Revelation 22:6–15 Revealed

To reassure John that he was indeed receiving a vision from God, Christ says in verse 6 that these words are faithful and true. He wants John, as well as the future readers of the book, to know that the record of the words in the book can be trusted and that John's accounts of the future are accurate. The words of this book can be tested to be true because the God of spirits who spoke through the prophets is the one who sent the angel to confirm these to John through a vision.

Christ then reminds us in verse 7 that He is coming quickly, so we must heed the words of this prophecy and keep our gaze fixed on eternity, because all these things will soon take place. Then in verses 8–10, John recounts the time in Chapter 19 verse 10 when he attempted to worship the angel who showed him the vision and he was rebuked quickly. It's a reminder that only God deserves our worship and that we should never elevate any messenger of God, whether a man or an angel, more than need be.

It's also important to note that the angel tells John not to seal up the vision because the time for these things to come to pass is soon.

Then the angel also gives John a sobering truth in verse 11, and that is that unbelievers will continue to live sinfully, and those who are righteous will continue to live righteously. Those who know the truth of Jesus Christ will continue to live and bear the fruit of a believer, and unless the unbeliever is convicted by the Holy Spirit, they are to be left to their devices.

From verses 12 to 15, Christ gives a final call to both believers and unbelievers, informing us that He is coming quickly and has rewards to give every man according to his deeds. He then gives a special salutation to those who have been cleansed by the blood of Jesus. Only these will have access to the tree of life and will be able to enter the gates of the Holy City.

On the contrary, he makes a distinction for those who will remain outside, namely, those who refuse to repent and believe and continue living the life of an unbeliever.

Revelation 22:16–21 Revealed

In the final few verses of Chapter 22, Jesus Himself is speaking, confirming that He has sent His angel to confirm the things in the book to the church. He is speaking directly to the reader in these verses, something He has done in no other book of the Bible.

Verse 17 says the Spirit and the bride say, "Come!" which means an invitation to faith in Jesus. He invites those who are thirsty for righteousness to come and drink from the water of life without cost.

In the following verse, Christ gives a stern warning not to change the words of the Scripture. He guarantees that anyone who does alter the Scripture will experience the torments written therein, in addition to being cast into the lake of fire. With so many false doctrines and heavily revised versions of the Bible in the world today, we can understand why the Lord would be so sensitive about His Word being altered. People's souls are at risk of being deceived and led to torment when words from the Bible are changed or handled carelessly.

He gives another strong warning in verse 19, assuring that if anyone takes away from the words of the prophecies of the Book of Revelation, He will remove them from the Holy City and from the Book of Life. But despite singling out the Book of Revelation, the warning extends to all the books of the Bible.

He then reaffirms in Revelation 22:20 that He is coming quickly. And by the looks of the prophecies happening in our world today, we can have confidence in His words.

As is the custom of many of the New Testament books, verse 21 ends with, "The grace of the Lord Jesus be with God's people. Amen."

End-of-Chapter Quiz

1. What is the name of the tree in the Holy City whose leaves are for the healing of the nation that was first in the Garden of Eden?
2. How many types of fruit does the tree of life bear?
3. What rebellious act caused God to curse the ground in the Book of Genesis?
4. Why are we told in verse 5 that there will be no night and no need for the sun or light in the new earth?
5. What does Christ warn will happen to anyone who adds to the words of prophecy spoken in the Book of Revelation?

Answers

1. The tree of life is the name of the tree that was once first in the Garden of Eden, and its leaves are used for healing among the nations of the new earth.
2. The tree of life bears 12 fruits, a different one for each month.
3. When Adam and Eve disobeyed God and ate from the tree of the knowledge of good and evil, He cursed the ground, which resulted in hard labor and toil, sickness, and physical death.
4. There will be no night or need for the sun in the new earth because the glory of the Lord will be an eternal source of light.
5. To anyone who adds to the words of the prophecy in the Book of Revelation, Jesus promises to add to him the plagues described in the scroll.

CONCLUSION

The Book of Revelation is one of the most, if not the most, popular books of the Bible. But just as it is popular, it is also one of the most misunderstood books as well, and we can see why! The imagery being used to describe what was seen is being written by John, a man who received in-depth visions of the future, including our present time and beyond, while living in 95. As we dissected the Book of Revelation line upon line and precept upon precept, we did our utmost to take the texts in their simplest form, unless otherwise proven. This is where many people go wrong and end up complicating the scriptures, their congregations, and themselves. It's for this reason that only someone who is filled with and led by the Holy Spirit should begin the journey of understanding the messages in this book.

Another reason that even believers shy away from reading the Book of Revelation is because it is filled with dark and often unpleasant realities that those with faith in Jesus Christ will have to face. Many of those dark truths are staring us in the face today as the world drifts further away from God and embraces a hedonistic, pagan life. Truly, when Jesus said in John 3:19, "This is the verdict: Light has come into the world, but people loved darkness instead of light because their deeds were evil." The intolerance for the Word of God in government, schools, and society at large is the reason mankind seems to be sliding down the proverbial razor blade into a cesspool of sin.

The very first chapter lets us know that the kingdom of God is near, despite being written over 2,000 years ago. While the letters were addressed to the seven churches in Asia, there is a lesson each genuine believer can take away from those passages of the Scripture. As believers, we never want to become complacent in our walk with Christ, as there is always something that we can learn and grow from spiritually. Even if you are part of a church organization and can apply some of the admonition to your church body, it's key to also use these scriptures to examine your own walk with Christ, since that is truly what will matter when you stand before the Lord.

The reason the Book of Revelation is such a fascinating read is because of the way it connects to other Old Testament books in the Bible, from Genesis and Deuteronomy to Isaiah and Daniel. It only serves as further proof that the Bible does not and cannot contradict itself. Rather, it confirms itself, leading us to marvel at both the intricacy and simplicity of God's Word. If you're a believer reading this book, it should give you a newfound respect and admiration for the Lord to know that after giving His life to redeem the Jewish people back to God the Father (and believing Gentiles by extension), He has prepared so much in the hereafter for those who truly love Him.

But as we are aware, many of us are to be tried and tested before experiencing the goodness God has prepared for us, which is why the tribulation period is there. Most born-again believers are focused on making it in the rapture of the Church, as we should be striving to. But the Bible makes it clear that some will be martyred for their faith during this intense tribulation period which will be the greatest test of faith for many who call themselves Christians. In the case of some of the natural disasters, such as the opening of some of the seven seals, the seven trumpets, and the bowl judgments, we may be affected but nonetheless protected from harm as we're promised in 2 Peter 2:9.

But the real danger comes when the Antichrist is revealed. The first five seals let us know the extent of the chaos that he will cause in the earth, all orchestrated by the Antichrist. The most trying time will be after Satan is cast out of heaven and no longer has access to the throne of God. He will make it his mission to persecute and terrorize the Jews and the people of God with oppression of all kinds, including economic and spiritual.

By instituting the mark of the beast, Satan in the form of the Antichrist will force the world to accept his mark in order to operate in daily life. Additionally, he will seek to force the saints to deny their faith in Christ by setting up an image of himself to be worshiped as a deity. And the penalty for refusing to submit to both his economic system and his spiritual practice will be death. This is why we are encouraged to be faithful to the point of death so that we will receive the crown of life.

If anyone knows about being faithful to the Lord, I do! Like many believers, I have searched feverishly for the truth throughout my life.

Raised as a Methodist and taught by my grandfather who was a minister in the Methodist Church, I would later become a Lutheran after being married. However, after my divorce, I was invited to the Catholic Church and have been going there ever since—for the past 20 years, actually! I believe that no true follower of Christ can say they've "arrived." The Bible is the living word, and therefore, as we live out our Christian walk, there are always new dimensions and fresh revelation to be discovered. And for me, that's the joy of it all —no pun intended.

I hope you will do the same on your journey in Christ. God loves a willing vessel, and if you are willing to learn even the uncomfortable truth about the gospel, I believe you'll be fully equipped for the times we're living in and what's to come. Despite the dark stuff, we have so many wonderful blessings and promises to look forward to in Christ. Keep the faith alive! And don't forget to leave a review on Amazon if you have found this book in any way helpful to your Christian walk or simply to better understand the Book of Revelation. Thank you in advance.

May God's blessings upon you be continuously overflowing in all realms of life, in this world, and in the one to come. And although there are events described in this book that are both fantastic and frightening, rest assured that while we may experience tribulation in this world, be of good cheer, because Christ has overcome the world!

HOW YOU CAN HELP SOMEONE ELSE

The Book of Revelation can be a difficult read for even those of firm faith. Now that you've deepened your understanding and welcomed a life of growth and revelation, you're in the perfect position to help others do the same.

Simply by leaving your honest opinion of this book on Amazon, you'll show new readers where they can find the guidance they need to better understand the Book of Revelation and welcome God's love into their lives.

LEAVE A REVIEW!

Thank you for helping me spread the word of God. When we work together, we can bring His light to the lives of many.

Scan the QR code for a quick review!

REFERENCES

Armstrong, S. (2019a, September 11). *Revelation 2020 - Lesson 1.* Verse by Verse Ministry International. https://versebyverseministry.org/lessons/revelation-2020-lesson-1

Armstrong, S. (2019b, September 11). *Revelation 2020 - Lesson 2A.* Verse by Verse Ministry International. https://versebyverseministry.org/lessons/revelation-2020-lesson-2a

Armstrong, S. (2019c, September 25). *Revelation 2020 - Lesson 2B.* Verse by Verse Ministry International. https://versebyverseministry.org/lessons/revelation-2020-lesson-2b

Armstrong, S. (2019d, October 2). *Revelation 2020 - Lesson 3.* Verse by Verse Ministry International. https://versebyverseministry.org/lessons/revelation-2020-lesson-3

Armstrong, S. (2019e, November 20). *Revelation 2020 - Lesson 6.* Verse by Verse Ministry International. https://versebyverseministry.org/lessons/revelation-2020-lesson-6a

God's word is meant to be shared. (2017, February 20). CSB. https://csbible.com/gods-word-meant-shared/

King James Bible. (2017). King James Bible Online. https://www.kingjamesbibleonline.org/ (Original work published 1611)

New International Version. (2011). Bible Study Tools. https://www.biblestudytools.com/ (Original work published 1973)

Riggleman, H. (2022, January 24). *What are the seven spirits of God?* Crosswalk. https://www.crosswalk.com/faith/bible-study/what-are-the-seven-spirits-of-god.html

Made in the USA
Middletown, DE
26 August 2024

59281452R00149